The *Effective Editor's Handbook*

The Effective Editor's Handbook

Barbara Horn

A copy of the British Library Cataloguing in Publication data is available on request.

ISBN 1 85802 186 3

First published in the UK in 1997 by
Pira International
Randalls Road
Leatherhead
Surrey
KT22 7RU
UK
Tel: (+44) (0) 1372 802080
Fax: (+44) (0) 1372 802079
E-mail: publications@pira.co.uk
http: //www.pira.co.uk/

Library of Congress Cataloging in Publication Data
(registration submitted October 1997)

Printed in the UK by Antony Rowe, Chippenham, Wilts

For Bob

Contents

Figures and tables   viii

Foreword   ix

Preface   xi

Acknowledgements   xiii

1   Editors: what's in a name?   1

2   Effective commissioning   7

3   From proposal to manuscript   31

4   Effective project management   43

5   Effective copy-editing   59

6   Working with designers   81

7   Working with picture researchers   101

8   Working with production   115

9   Working with freelancers   129

10   Copyright and permissions   145

11   Working with marketing, sales and promotion   159

Glossary   169

Index   171

Figures and tables

Table 2.1	Outlining the characteristics of the list	8
Figure 2.1	The basis of a proposal, relating income to expenditure	11
Figure 2.2	Using mark-up to calculate price and unit cost	13
Figure 2.3	A global schedule form, with external events marked	17
Figure 2.4	Typical editorial and design fixed costs	26
Figure 3.1	An example of a handover form for use by editors and designers	40–1
Figure 4.1	A traditional production schedule for an illustrated book	48
Figure 4.2	A DTP production schedule for an illustrated book	48
Figure 4.3	A project manager's global schedule	50
Figure 5.1	A copy-editor's global schedule	64
Figure 6.1	A design brief	86
Figure 6.2	An artwork brief	90
Figure 6.3	Cover and jacket brief	94
Figure 7.1	Information to include in a picture research brief	102
Figure 7.2	A picture research contract	108–9
Figure 8.1	The book production processes	116
Figure 8.2	An estimate request form for an illustrated book	118-9
Figure 8.3	A production estimate form	122
Figure 8.4	A proof-return form	128
Figure 9.1	A freelancer's record	135
Figure 9.2	A checklist of tasks	138
Figure 10.1	Duration of copyright in literary, dramatic and artistic work	146–7
Figure 10.2	A template for recording sources	153
Figure 10.3	Example of a permission form letter from a publishing house	155

Foreword

Whatever the job status one achieves, the position one holds or the length of time within that role, everyone can improve upon their individual performance. While very few would disagree with that truth — after all they would be foolish so to do — it is generally the young, the newly appointed, or those with ambition that access the ways and means of developing their personal or occupational skills and abilities. There are, of course, many reasons why improving performance is difficult for some. A lack of time and work pressures are most commonly quoted, particularly by those who manage or supervise others.

There is an obvious danger in standing still in personal development terms, however, 'while all about change is taking place'. This is possibly more true in book publishing at this time than in any other sector. Not only is publishing having to come to grips with IT and the electronic publishing revolution to remain competitive, it is also suffering from a combination of weak markets and a perceived, though not necessarily acknowledged, fall in professional standards.

At the same time, the industry emphasis seems still to be to publish as many books as possible in order to achieve the required contribution, profit, share price or dividend, even if that means a sacrifice of quality. The real question is whether higher output necessarily means a deterioration in the product, and many have, and are, wrestling with this challenge.

One thing is certain. No matter how many books are published, and how fast the manufacturing process improves through the use of computer technology, the industry still relies on people to commission, acquire, edit and steer the manuscript through to finished book. They haven't yet developed the software to take on those roles!

I feel fairly certain that if those people — and let us give them their proper title of Editors — could improve their individual performance, even just a little, the return on that investment, both personally and for the company in which they work, could be considerable.

There is now a fairly simple, straightforward and time-saving way in which that improvement could be effected. By keeping a copy of this book on your desk and referring to it at those times when you are tempted to say, 'there must be a better/easier way of doing this', or, 'I suppose I am doing it the right way', improvement in working practices will result.

For those new to editing, this book should sit alongside Judith Butcher's *Copy-editing* and the *Oxford Dictionary for Writers and Editors*. Every aspect of the editorial function is covered in detail together with a professional standard by which one can measure one's effectiveness.

For the relatively inexperienced to the 'old-hand', every editor can be assured of gaining a lot of valuable information, guidance and practical help from *The Effective Editor's Handbook*.

Dag Smith
Publishing Training Centre, Book House

Preface

There are books devoted to book commissioning and many manuals and style guides for copy-editing. This book is not one of them. Its purpose is to show how editors who have learned the basic skills can employ them so that they make optimum use of time, money and effort, establish and maintain good working relationships with colleagues, avoid stress and prevent unnecessary crises in producing good books.

What is a good book? From the economic point of view, it is one that will sell out its print run in a specified period of time at a profit, and will then continue to sell as a reprint, a backlist book, a money-maker. Therefore, it is a book that people want or need, at a price they are willing to pay, produced at a price/cost ratio that results in an acceptable margin of profit, and on a schedule that does not tie up the capital investment for too long before the sales can create income. From a purely qualitative point of view, a book is considered to be good if it is perceived and praised as one that makes a valuable contribution to its field or genre in its content, literary style, illustration, design or production. Idealists may think that these two types of goodness should always combine in a book, but the reality is that they do not: some bestsellers are poorly constructed, badly written or derivative, or poorly edited, illustrated, designed or produced, but they are what a particular market wants at a price it is willing to pay. Some books that are original or have high editorial, design or production values do not make money. Everyone is happy when a book is a bestseller, of course, but publishers do not automatically despair when a good-quality book fails to make a good profit — at least, not if they were aware of that outcome before they decided to publish — for their goal may have been reached in providing important information or laying the foundation for later success by the same author. Looked at in this way, a good book is one that performs as expected; a very good book exceeds expectation.

To produce good books, then, editors have to know what is expected not only of the book but also of them. Their jobs are multifaceted and vary according to where they work, and Chapter 1 matches the titles editors are given to the main tasks for which they are responsible. Because the division of labour differs from house to house and because we should all have an understanding of what the entire editorial process is so that we can work more effectively, the remaining chapters are intended to be read by all editors, regardless of their title. The next two chapters look at the ways in which commissioning editors can produce proposals that satisfy the company's expectations, and work with authors so that the manuscripts they write can efficiently be turned into the books that were proposed. Chapter 4 examines how to determine the most appropriate way to manage projects after they have been commissioned, and Chapter 5 focuses on how to approach copy-editing the text, from assessing and scheduling the job to working with authors and briefing indexers.

Too often in publishing there are obstacles to communication between editors, designers and production controllers. These are the barriers of ignorance and prejudice. There are editors who regard everyone whose job is not verbally oriented as a lesser being; designers who consider editors and production controllers ignorant meddlers in the creative process; and production controllers who see editors and designers as prodigal impediments to producing books on time and within budget. Each group knows that the books cannot be produced without it, but some individuals fail to recognize that the books cannot be produced through their contribution alone. To work effectively with other people, you must understand and respect what they do, and know how and when your jobs interrelate. Chapters 6–8 explain the roles of designers, picture researchers and production controllers, and suggest how to develop the most beneficial working relationship with these colleagues.

The specific concerns of working with freelancers are addressed in Chapter 9. All editors deal with copyright to some extent, whether in contracts with authors and other publishers or in clearing permissions or checking that clearance has been obtained and preparing the acknowledgements. The general principles that govern this area are covered in Chapter 10. The last chapter focuses on the role that editors play in helping to promote and sell the book.

Some of the points made in the text will probably confirm what you know and what you do. Others may make you question what you do and offer you new information or alternative ways of approaching certain tasks. It is always important to view suggestions and advice from the perspective of, and, if necessary, adapt them to, the specific circumstances in which you work. If you find aspects of the way you work that you want to change, do not try to revolutionize yourself overnight; make a list of priorities and plan for gradual and incremental change so that you can achieve your objectives calmly, in an organized manner and without adding stress to your life.

Being a good communicator is emphasized in every chapter, for a willingness and ability to communicate with everyone involved in the publishing process is fundamental to being an effective editor. It enables us not only to do our present job well, but also to take advantage of the opportunity that editorial work offers to continue learning throughout our career, to expand and improve our skills so that we can meet the challenges presented by the economic and technological changes in our industry, and to derive the maximum satisfaction from our work — benefits that for many of us compensate for the generally low rates of pay.

Acknowledgements

This book is the result of experience, a shared process. I have learned a great deal from, and am grateful to, so many people with whom I have worked. It is not possible to thank them all individually here, but there is one person who must be mentioned, a man who made an indelible impression on me and, I believe, all those who have been fortunate enough to know him. It has been a particular privilege to know and to have worked for Jeff Bevington, whose deep concern for books and readers, authors and editors, for quality and honesty and humanity was evident in his every act.

I have also learned a great deal from and am grateful to the authors of other and more detailed guides to the various aspects of publishing, particularly David Bann, *Book Production Control* (Pira International, 1995) and *The Print Production Handbook* (rev. edn, Little, Brown, 1997); Judith Butcher, *Copy-editing* (3rd edn, CUP, 1992); Alastair Campbell, *The Designer's Handbook* (Macdonald, 1983); *The Chicago Manual of Style* (14th edn, University of Chicago Press, 1993); Gill Davies, *Book Commissioning and Acquisition* (Blueprint, 1995); and Michael F. Flint, *A User's Guide to Copyright* (4th edn, Butterworths, 1997).

In bringing this book to fruition, I am especially indebted to the following people for giving so generously of their time and expertise in making improvements to the text: Richard Balkwill for his comments on Chapters 1–4 and 10; David Bann for his advice on Chapter 8 and for allowing me to adapt the estimate request and estimate forms from his book *Book Production Control*; Elizabeth Bland for her general support and for her advice on Chapters 4 and 5; Gillian Clarke for her empathy for a novice author and her useful comments on Chapter 9; Cathy Douglas for her astute additions to Chapter 11; Richard Johnson for his helpful observations on Chapter 6; and Julia Pashley for her advice on Chapter 7.

My special thanks to Dag Smith of the Publishing Training Centre at Book House for suggesting the book to me and introducing me to Pira International; to him, Jean Hindmarch and Orna O'Brien, for giving me many opportunities as a tutor to develop my ideas; and to Ingmar Folkmans, Lewis Marshall, Jennifer Skelley, Ruth Freestone King, Milan Taylor and Jeff Archer of Pira International, for treating me with the care and consideration that every author would be delighted to receive.

My final and everlasting thanks are to Bob, who encouraged me in this endeavour, helped me through my frustrations and doubts, and continues to make the sun shine.

1
Editors: what's in a name?

In most industries and professions, job titles describe an occupation and may indicate a specialized area of activity and status. In book publishing, editorial job titles do not always perform these functions clearly. They depend not only on the jobs people do but also on where they do them. Editors can work in book publishing houses; in the publishing arm of academic, trade, professional and charitable organizations; and freelance. Editorial assistants in one firm might be called junior editors or assistant editors in another, while some organizations have a hierarchy that includes both editorial assistants and assistant editors. Similarly, 'senior editor', 'desk editor' and 'project editor' might describe a similar job in three different houses, commissioning editors here might be called publishers there, and the responsibilities of the editorial director in one house might be quite different from those of the person bearing the same title in another. The term 'editor' used alone does not indicate which of the editorial activities the holder performs or whether he or she does them all. Laying a foundation for clear communication, the text below outlines the various editorial jobs and discusses the titles that are most commonly used to describe each one.

The list-builders

Editorial work divides into two broad areas, the first of which is deciding what to publish. The 'glamour' of our supposedly glamorous industry lies in the image of the editors who 'discover' new authors, take them to lunch, nurture them into writing bestsellers, mingle with celebrities at launch parties, and go to lunch some more. Like many images, this one is composed of solid fact and wishful thinking.

Complete manuscripts or synopses and sample chapters can be submitted to publishing houses by authors or agents, and certain editors have the job of deciding which ones should be published by their firm and negotiating the terms for the right to do so. The majority of new fiction is acquired in this way. Some editors have the job of originating ideas for books and finding and commissioning authors to write the manuscripts. The majority of nonfiction is commissioned. From this description you might begin to think that one kind of editor is called an acquisitions editor and the other is called a commissioning editor. However, the first kind of editor also commissions, the second kind sometimes selects a complete manuscript that has been submitted, and both types might buy the rights to publish a paperback edition of a hardback book published by another house or the right to publish a translation of a book written in another language. The distinction between the job titles, therefore, tends to be national rather than functional: in Britain, for example, both kinds of editor tend to be called commissioning editors, and in the United States they tend to be called acquisitions editors. They might also be called publishers or editorial directors, but these are less helpful titles because they are used to describe other jobs too. The publisher, for example, may be a person who sets the strategy for the list and controls the overall budget but does not personally select which titles to acquire or which authors to commission, and the editorial director may be head of the department that processes the manuscripts but is not responsible for acquiring them.

Regardless of their title, these list-building editors must have a clear understanding of the type(s) of book that their company can publish effectively, how each prospective title will fit into the list; what the market for that book wants and expects in terms of content, quality and price; how to produce it; and the nature of the competition. Success depends on more than the talent for spotting the right idea at the right moment, or 'flair'. It requires awareness not simply of what is in the market, of how well it sells and why, but also of gaps, however sliver thin, and of new trends. Depending on the editor's particular area of publishing, that means reading articles and reviews; watching television, listening to the radio, and going to films and live performances; attending conferences, seminars, book fairs and exhibitions; visiting bookshops and educational and academic institutions. The lunches for which editors are so well known, and frequently envied or criticized by their sandwich-munching colleagues, provide the optimum environment for sounding out potential new authors, for discussing new ideas with existing authors and advisers, for establishing and maintaining relationships with agents, consultants and other publishers, and for the sometimes hard work of negotiating with them.

Becoming an adept communicator is essential for selling the ideas to colleagues; for encouraging and supporting authors during the writing and, if necessary, the revision processes; for briefing those who will turn the manuscript into a book; and for promoting the book, the author and the list.

The 'back-room' workers

The second broad area of editorial work is in making the manuscript into a book. Not only is this side of editorial work not glamorous, but generally few people outside publishing, and not everyone within, understands what it involves. The kind and extent of activities vary according to the type of publishing, the house and the individual's level of experience, as do the job titles, although generically the work is referred to as copy-editing.

The aim of copy-editing is to make the author's message easily and clearly accessible to the reader. The tasks involved in achieving this goal range from correcting grammar and spelling, imposing house style, and checking text and illustrations for accuracy, consistency and relevance to reorganizing, restructuring and rewriting. They may include clearing permissions to use copyright material; researching photographs and artwork; briefing designers, illustrators, picture researchers, photographers and indexers; cutting and filling text; and writing captions. Sometimes writing jacket or cover blurbs, advance information sheets and catalogue copy is the job of the commissioning editor, sometimes that of the copy-editor, and often a collaborative effort.

All copy-editors have to be able to proofread. It is usually the first training that editorial assistants are given because it shows them what a copy-editor has done, and thus gives them an opportunity to learn editorial skills by example. However, not all proofreaders become copy-editors, and the purpose of proofreading is not to edit the manuscript again, although by correcting errors and raising queries it tidies up the editing and can indicate where more work needs to be done.

Copy-editing requires a great deal of knowledge and skill, initiative and self-discipline, meticulous attention to detail, an open mind, good organization and excellent communication skills. The most general term for people who do this job in book publishing is copy-editor. Some publishing houses use 'subeditor', which is more common in magazine, journal and newspaper publishing. 'Production editor' signifies a copy-editor who also has the responsibility for controlling the pre-press stages of production, from typesetting and origination to page make-up and film. Production editors are usually found in journal publishing, where every issue follows the same style, and the same typesetter and printer are always used, but they also work in houses that produce books in only a few formats.

The terms 'assistant', 'associate', 'senior' and 'director', which can be affixed to either commissioning editors or copy-editors, indicate position in the hierarchy in a particular firm, but do not necessarily reflect experience or competence, or even indicate the size or organization of the editorial department. For example, editorial assistant is usually the most junior editorial job, a position in which a person learns the basic skills and may do secretarial and administrative work for a higher-level editor. However, in some firms people might retain the title 'editorial assistant' for a prolonged period because there is no policy for assessing and rewarding development, because there are no vacancies for promotion, or even because it is a way for the company to get the higher level of work without paying a higher salary. In other firms editorial assistants might be promoted after a set time in the job whether or not they are competent.

A house may have such a small staff that there are no editorial assistants, only experienced editors, who may be called simply editors or project, desk or senior editors. These editors may do the copy-editing themselves or may delegate it to other copy-editors while supervising and coordinating the work between individuals and departments. Managing editors oversee a company's workload — or in very large organizations, the workload of an imprint, division or list — distributing manuscripts to other editors, in-house or freelance, and controlling the schedules. Managing editors do not always attain this position because they are highly experienced or good copy-editors; sometimes their organizational skills are considered more important. Those skills certainly are essential. However, the goal is not only to get books out on time, but also to make sure that they are of the specified quality and produced within the budget. To fulfil those criteria, managing editors need a sound foundation in copy-editing, for this is what enables them to select the appropriate people for each job, brief them and check the work.

Overlap and crossover

Some editors acquire or commission books and copy-edit them, but most people do not have the time, the skill or the inclination to do both. Commissioning editors view the large picture: the current market and future trends; the list over the next three- to five-year period; the subject and structure of individual books. They create the budgets, specify the target audience, and in some cases — particularly in illustrated nonfiction — determine the book's physical specifications. To do their job well, they have to be out of the office a great deal of the time, researching, discussing, interacting with people. Creative, imaginative, energetic and loquacious are words frequently used to describe people drawn to this kind of work.

Copy-editing is not a stage on the route to commissioning, although understanding what it involves might be useful in that job and some copy-editors do become list-builders. Copy-editors view the smaller picture, focusing on the manuscripts allocated to them, their budgets, schedules and specifications, the details of their texts and illustrations, and the needs and expectations of their targeted audiences.

To do their job well, they have to spend a lot of time in an office — their own or the publisher's — liaising with authors and interacting with editorial, design and production colleagues. Meticulous, patient, practical and inquisitive are common descriptions of copy-editors.

Both commissioning editors and copy-editors may play a part in the budget and schedule, in developing the author, in shaping the manuscript, and in producing materials for sales, rights and promotion. Therefore, for each of them to work effectively, there must be good communication between them. In an ideal world the commissioning editor briefs the copy-editor on the proposal, the copy-editor provides feedback on estimated editorial costs and time; the commissioning editor briefs the copy-editor on the author and the manuscript, the copy-editor provides feedback on how the editorial stages are progressing and how the author is reacting; either one initiates the jacket or cover copy, the catalogue blurb and the advance information sheet, the other checks it and provides feedback. Of course, our world is often far from ideal, but the ideal is our goal, and we can work towards it now that we know what it is.

The wider network

As well as working with each other and with authors, commissioning editors and copy-editors must, at different times and to differing degrees, liaise with all the other people involved in the publishing process. In the beginning, it will be seen, the commissioning editor must communicate with sales, marketing and rights, perhaps with readers and advisers, and with design and production to produce viable proposals. In the subsequent stages copy-editors work with other editorial personnel, such as proofreaders and indexers, and with design, production, rights, sales, marketing and promotion to produce the titles in the way the commissioning editors have envisaged them. Since it is editors who initiate the projects, who are involved in more stages of production and are more verbally oriented than their colleagues in the other departments, it is they who should take the initiative, asking for information when they need it and offering information that others might need without waiting to be asked.

Communication is an essential tool of leadership. It provides the control that editors need to enable projects to come to fruition on time, within budget and to the required standard without avoidable crises. Communication, whether of stories or information, is the purpose of publishing, and therefore it is surprising how often the lack of it is responsible for the problems we encounter in our work. You may have great ideas, flair, or all the basic copy-editing skills, but without the ability to communicate clearly and appropriately, you cannot and will not be an effective editor.

Effective meetings

Casual meetings in the corridor or at the coffee machine or photocopier are opportunities to exchange simple information and pleasantries, but it is better to arrange more formal meetings for prolonged discussion on complex or sensitive issues. Follow the same procedure whether the meeting is with colleagues in-house or people outside. Contact the person or people involved, tell them the purpose of the proposed meeting, estimate the length of time it will take, and suggest a time and a place. Obviously, the meeting will be easier to arrange if you contact the other parties a reasonable amount of time in advance and are prepared to suggest a number of alternative dates and times.

Choosing the most appropriate environment contributes to a meeting's success. Meetings with people from outside the company are often conducted over lunch, whereas most meetings with colleagues take place in-house. Try to arrange your meetings in a place and at a time where you are least likely to be disturbed or distracted. A meeting room is ideal because you will not be interrupted by people walking in or telephoning (turn off your mobile phone). If it has to be in your office or in the office of one of your colleagues, close the door and arrange not to be interrupted by telephone calls: have them answered by an assistant or other colleague or by voice-mail system if it is available. If the meeting has to take place in an open-plan area, let people know that you do not want to be disturbed, and discourage anyone from interrupting you by avoiding eye contact. If someone persists and you ascertain that the issue is not urgent, explain quietly and as briefly as possible that you are in a meeting and will be available later. When you see that person later, it might be necessary, depending on the individual's experience, to reiterate that meetings should be interrupted only for urgent matters and even to explain what might be an urgent matter and what types of issue can wait. Such constructive feedback can benefit the individual, whose more discriminating behaviour will serve him or her well generally, and you and your colleagues, whose meetings will not be interrupted.

2

Effective commissioning

Books are born of ideas, and it is your responsibility to choose the ideas that will make good books for your company. Imagination and the oft-mentioned flair are important assets, for without imagination, there are no new ideas, and without flair, the potential of a manuscript, a trend or an opportunity may be missed. But not every good idea will result in a good book for a particular house, and not every commissioning editor has both or either of these innate qualities to the same degree, if at all. You can work on a successful list without ever having a new idea of your own. You might depend on specialists in a particular field to advise you on what needs to be published, or you might take your inspiration from other publishers' successes, following trends rather than setting them. Whether the ideas are new or derivative, your own or another's, you need to assure yourself and convince your colleagues that they will make potentially good books. That requires research, analysis and communication.

Getting to know you

To be effective, you have to balance what the market wants with what your publishing house can deliver. In order to do that, you must first familiarize yourself with the list. If it is a complex one, making a table of the subject areas or genres and their qualities (see Table 2.1) might help you to answer the following questions.

- Does the list have a coherent pattern or is it a collection of very loosely related parts?
- Is it balanced or are some areas under- or over-represented?
- Are there noticeable gaps?

  The next set of questions arises from the answers to the first.
- If the list is unorganized, what are your responsibilities and priorities for organizing it?

Table 2.1 Outlining the characteristics of the list

Subject	No. of titles	Age range	Knowledge level	Format mm inches	Extent PP	Market range	Sales area
Culinary arts							
reference							
dict'y of vegetables	1	adult	beginner	295 × 225 $11\frac{1}{2} \times 8\frac{3}{4}$	128	mid	trade
dict'y of cheese	1	adult	beginner	295 × 225 $11\frac{1}{2} \times 8\frac{3}{4}$	128	up	trade
techniques	1	adult	experienced home cook	295 × 225 $11\frac{1}{2} \times 8\frac{3}{4}$	192	up	trade
Recipes							
individual foods	6	adult	beginner	200 × 165 8×6	64	down	trade
cakes	1	adult	beginner	295 × 225 $11\frac{1}{2} \times 8\frac{3}{4}$	224	mid	trade
individual foods	6	adult	experienced home cook	270 × 230 $10\frac{1}{2} \times 9$	176	mid	direct mail
confectionery	1	adult	experienced/professional	270 × 230 $10\frac{1}{2} \times 9$	256	up	trade

- If it is unbalanced, is that the result of planning or accident, and are you expected to build up the slim areas or trim the fat ones, or vice versa?
- Are any glaring gaps a matter of policy or are you expected to fill them?

Perhaps some of this ground was covered when you were appointed to the job or perhaps your brief is to make this analysis and your plan for building the list your first task. In the unhappy event that neither of these possibilities describes your situation, analyse the list now.

A close look at the foundations

When you have assessed the nature of the list and its pattern or lack of one, get an accurate picture of the past sales performance. Study the sales records to learn which titles sold as well or better than expected and which did not, then talk to the sales and marketing departments to find out their view of why this was so.

To get the maximum information in the minimum amount of time, prepare yourself and give your colleagues a chance to prepare too. Compare individual books on your lists of good and poor sellers with your tabular analysis: do you see any obvious reason for their performance? Read reviews in the files. Use a checklist of specifications to help you get a thorough picture of apparent strengths and weaknesses. It might include some of the following points, depending on the kinds of book the company publishes:

- subject and particular approach
- level of information
- language level
- index
- academic apparatus
- format
- extent
- design
- number and style of illustrations
- use of colour
- price

    Include marketing issues, such as:
- impact of authors' names and credentials,
- tie-in to TV, film or other events,
- seasonal qualifications,
- how and where sales were promoted.

Analyse this information to determine if there is a simple pattern. See if you can organize the titles into groups based on common characteristics and performance. If there are a small number of titles that do not fit into the pattern, see if they have anything in common with each other.

Checking out the competition

Your conclusions will be based on the books seen in isolation. The responses you want to get from sales and marketing should reveal what role these and other factors played in the various titles' competition with books from other publishers. For example, to what extent was the books' market share a reflection of:

- their perceived value for money,
- the authors' status,
- the timing of publication,
- targeting the right readers,
- the nature and extent of promotion,
- the strength of the competition?

If your company has several lists, read the catalogue to see if there are potential areas of overlap or conflict; it is difficult enough competing with other firms without competing with your own.

When you make an appointment to see the relevant individuals, tell them the nature of the background information you are seeking and ask their opinion of how much time they will need in order to make the picture clear to you. Allow a little longer. At your meeting introduce each title or group of titles with your own concise evaluation, then ask your colleagues if they concur with or have a different view on each point. This might sound tedious, but otherwise you could end up with a comment on the extent of one and the subject of another, but no consistent information overall. If you number the points, you will find it quicker and easier to make sure that you have covered all of them each time, to vary the order in which you raise them so that the procedure is not monotonous, and to make notes. Remember, the information you get from sales and marketing is their informed perspective. You have to balance their feedback with your own initial evaluation and then examine the competition to get a complete picture.

Look at your competitors' lists to see in what ways they outshine your company's publications. Do they cover the subject field more widely, in greater depth, with more prominent authors? Notice the visual and physical presentations, and the prices: what makes them seem good or better value? Remember to look at the covers or jackets too.

- Do the fronts do a better job of attracting your attention?
- Are the blurbs better at asserting the value of the books?
- Do they include better or different promotional devices?
- Do they utilize the space better?

Check the appropriate sources for advertisements and reviews. Do your competitors' books seem to get better coverage? For trade books, look at their presence in bookshops. Do they, for example, have their own special shelving or permanent display stands, eye-catching point-of-sale materials or promotional gimmicks?

Summarize and digest all this information to get an image of how well your list has been performing in the face of competition, and why.

Budget principles

The next questions you have to ask are:

1 Did those titles that sold well make an acceptable margin of profit?
2 Did any of the titles that sold poorly in the main domestic market make an acceptable profit margin as a result of income from subsidiary rights?
3 How could any of the books that sold poorly because they were perceived as overpriced have been produced more economically?
4 Did any of the titles perform less well than expected because they were published late?

Before you can answer these questions you need to know how the company determines the profit margin and what it considers an acceptable level. Most houses have a form for the financial side of proposals that relates the proposed expenditure to the estimated income. There are many variations on the detail, but the general elements are the same. These are summarized in Figure 2.1.

```
      RSP − discount
  ×   print run − freebies
  =   turnover
  +   rights income
  =   total income
  −   direct costs
  =   gross profit margin
  −   overheads
  =   net profit margin before tax and interest
```

Figure 2.1 The basis of a proposal, relating income to expenditure

The retail sales price (RSP) is how you position the book in the market, but it is not the money the publisher receives, except for books sold by direct mail. For all other sales, the publisher sells the books at a discount, which allows the intermediaries — wholesalers and retailers — to cover their costs and make a profit too. The turnover is not generated by the total print run; some copies — commonly called 'freebies' because they are free of charge to their users — are given to the author, sent out for review or inspection, carried by sales representatives, used by the rights department, and kept as reprint and file copies.

To the turnover can be added income from the sales of co-editions, book-club editions, extracts, serials and other subsidiary rights. These revenues must be guaranteed if they are to be included in the calculation at this point; many books are not candidates for extraction or serialization, for example, while some firms sell co-editions and book-club editions before approving a proposal and spending money. Having estimated the total income for the print run, you have to subtract the costs of producing the book.

Direct costs are those incurred in producing a specific book and therefore always include the manufacturing costs (see Chapter 8) and authors' fees or royalties. Overheads generally refer to those costs of running the company that cannot be itemized title by title — salaries of everyone in the company, rent, insurance, utilities, equipment, maintenance, supplies, distribution and so on — and are calculated as a percentage of the turnover. In some houses, usually those that produce a large number of discrete titles, editorial and design work are allocated to direct costs to provide a more accurate unit cost for each title; in others, mainly those that publish a few limited formats, these costs may be categorized as investment overheads.

The ratio of the net profit margin to the total expenditure — that is, the percentage of return on the funds employed — will determine whether a proposal is acceptable. Profits are needed for investment in new projects and new equipment, to pay for additional staff and increases in the salaries of existing staff, and to pay taxes, interest on loans and dividends if there are shareholders. The company will have a target net profit margin but may accept a project that does not look likely to attain it. It might do this because it is developing an author whose subsequent book it believes will be a bestseller, because the book is important in its field and will contribute to the publisher's reputation or for some other marketing reason, and it will do this only in the knowledge that there are other titles that are exceeding the target and, in effect, supporting this one.

The mark-up is a shortcut, a quick guide to the relationship between the unit cost and the retail price (Figure 2.2). The unit cost is the cost of producing each copy, calculated by dividing the direct costs by the print run (see also Chapter 8). The mark-up is a factor that accounts for overheads and the acceptable net profit margin. Dividing the estimated retail price by the mark-up tells you the maximum unit cost allowable; multiplying the unit cost by the mark-up shows the necessary retail price.

$$\frac{\text{direct costs}}{\text{print run}} = \text{unit cost} \times \text{mark-up} = \text{RSP}$$

$$\frac{\text{RSP}}{\text{mark-up}} = \text{unit cost}$$

Figure 2.2 Using mark-up to calculate price and unit cost

Armed with this understanding, you should find the answers to the first two questions listed above easy to obtain: compare the estimate of costs and sales revenue on which the proposal was accepted to the actual amounts spent and received, and note the effect on the projected net profit margin. There may be a running account in the monthly sales figures, as well as the annual title-by-title analysis. The latter might also remind you to make an appointment to talk to the rights manager about why certain titles did or did not fulfil expectations in this area of sales.

To answer the third question, you need to look at the costs for the book, or a representative number of books, concerned.

- Were they above estimate, and if so, in what areas?
- Were there heavy correction costs, and if so, why?
- Were there additional design or manufacturing costs, and if so, was that because of poor briefing, changes in the specification or delays in the schedule?
- If the costs were in line with the estimate, could the work have been done more economically or the specification altered to produce a lower-priced book with the same perceived value?

The fourth question points out another relationship between budgets and schedules. Books that are published late lose sales. The amount of sales they lose might depend on the how critical the date is — coinciding with an event or seasonal celebration, for example — or the availability of competition. (See 'Effective scheduling', below, and Chapter 3 for your role in creating and maintaining schedules.) If titles were late, what were the reasons and is there a pattern?

Some people dislike this kind of review. 'Let's not hold a post-mortem, let's not blame anybody,' they say. However, the point of a post-mortem is not to find someone to blame, but to learn why the book failed and how you can plan to prevent the same problems from leading to the failure of other books. If particular individuals or systems have contributed to the failure, this is an opportunity to provide constructive feedback, and perhaps training, to the individuals and to look at ways of improving the systems.

You are paid to think

Even as I write I can hear a collective piercing cry: 'Good grief! I don't have time to do all that. I've got quotas to fill, budgets to compile, schedules to meet, meetings to attend. I'm too busy to think!' Well, if you don't do the planning, you will always be too busy to think. The result will be that you will find it more time-consuming and more difficult to fill those quotas with *good* books, increasingly difficult if not impossible to prepare and maintain sensible and realistic budgets and schedules, and stressful and frustrating to go to meetings because you are not well prepared. Thinking is a fundamental part of your job. Researching the list gives you essential background information about the strengths and weaknesses of the foundation on which you are going to build, the sales and marketing perspective on the general nature of the competition, and a basic understanding of how your firm operates. It should help you to plan your work, determine your priorities and avoid obvious pitfalls. Make time to do it in the beginning (see 'Effective scheduling', below) — it probably will not take as long as you fear — and you will save time, money and effort thereafter.

Planning for action

When you know what the company can do well, look at what you are expected to do.

- How many titles are you expected to commission or acquire each year?
- How many of them are intended to be published in the current year, the next year, the year after?
- What is your budget for revenues each year?
- What is your budget for expenditure each year?

Correlate the answers to these questions with what you know about the list to determine your priorities. For example, decide what proportion of your quota will be aimed at filling gaps, at strengthening weak areas and at maintaining strong areas. You might need to lay a strong foundation if the gap is large or use limited resources to plug a small one, but you must not ignore a gap or you will waste an opportunity to fortify the list. Even if the decision is made to drop some weak areas, there will still be some that are weaker than others. It might be tempting to put all your effort into the strong areas to try to ensure success, but that would increase any imbalance in the list, making your job more difficult later ... if you are still there later.

It is not the number of titles alone that will have an impact on the health of the list, but their type, a combination of editorial and design approach and physical specification. Depending on the diversity in your list, you have to consider, for example, how many of the titles devoted to the separate functions of gap-filling, strengthening and maintenance need to be broadly based or narrowly focused; long, short or in between; illustrated or unillustrated; high, middle or low quality and price; and long or short print run.

Work out how many titles of the various kinds need to be published in each year to achieve your target revenues and to have the desired effect on the functions. The first part is strictly arithmetical: x copies of y titles at price 1 plus x copies of y titles at price 2 plus x copies of y titles at price 3 will meet the budget. The second part takes more thought. For example, if you plug a small gap in the current year with several substantial titles, you might be able to build on this area in subsequent years with fewer major works. It might not be practicable to try to fill a large gap or revivify a weak area all at once, but you can plan to establish the basis for these activities in the current year and continue to add to it throughout your three-year plan.

You then have to examine your budget for expenditure and estimate how much of it will be allocated to fees for consultants and advisers, authors, expenses and direct costs to produce the number and kinds of book planned. You will set the budget for each book when you do your own proposals, but at this point you need to check that, generally, your financial resources appear sufficient to support your programme. It might help to look at an analysis of the previous year's budget, if it is available, or even a selection of recent proposal forms.

- Is this year's budget the same size as last year's?
- Is it meant to pay for developing and producing the same quantity, quality and variety of books?
- Has it allowed for increased costs?

If the budget does not look large enough for your needs, try to work out how great the shortfall is likely to be. If it is a small percentage, you may be able to accommodate it by careful planning. If it is a large percentage, you may have miscalculated, so check both it and your plan again. If the figures refuse to improve, approach your immediate superior now. A discussion on the finances you have to work with should explain any aspect you have overlooked or misinterpreted, make your superior aware of any miscalculation at his, her or a higher level, or make it clear what a challenge you are facing.

A never-ending task

To have a consistently strong list you have to keep track of how it is performing. Everyone likes to warm themselves in the glow of high sales figures, but remember to notice general shifts in performance too, then try to find out the reasons for them and revise your plans accordingly. If a previously strong area is weakening, you may be getting the first information about changes in the market. Perhaps there is greater competition in this area and price range than there was before; or perhaps, although your quality of production has remained up to standard, your editorial approach and design formats are becoming stale; or perhaps the subject is overexposed. Test your own assessment of the market by discussing it with sales and marketing.

Effective scheduling

Everyone in publishing works to schedules. Their purpose is to enable us to get all our work done to the required standard in normal working hours. If you do not schedule your activities, you will not be able to make the optimum use of your time and, as a result, you might have to work overtime to achieve your goals. You could also forget to do things at the right time or at all, and your failure could disrupt the work of other people, impair your working relationships and endanger the success of the project. Such eventualities are accompanied by stress, which you probably do not need or want and can avoid.

To schedule your time and activities effectively, you need to create an overview of the time you have available, just as you needed to make an overview of your publishing programme. You can buy a year-to-view calendar or create one easily on a piece of graph paper or on a computer (see Figure 2.3). Whatever form you use, make sure it is big enough to write legible notes on. Put it where you can see it easily or have quick access to it: attach it to a wall or carry it in your personal organizer, diary or date book.

Use a highlighter to mark all the public holidays in the year; these are days on which the office is closed and you plan not to work; it is people who do not plan who often have to work then. Use another highlighter to mark events that have some impact on your work but whose dates are outside your control, such as sales conferences and book fairs, symposia or conferences in your subject area, and term times and exam periods in the academic or school year. These are part of the framework within which you work. They indicate dates on which you might have to attend an event, by which you might have to have done certain work, or after which you expect to see reports; or they may identify periods when you know colleagues or agents or authors and potential authors will be particularly busy or available. Mark

Title and spec	Jan					Feb				Mar				Apr				May					June				July					Aug				Sept				Oct					Nov				Dec			
	2	9	16	23	30	6	13	20	27	6	13	20	27	3	10	17	24	1	8	15	22	29	5	12	19	26	3	10	17	24	31	7	14	21	28	4	11	18	25	2	9	16	23	30	6	13	20	27	4	11	18	25

External events marked (reading left to right): *New Year*, *Sales Conference*, *Bologna Book Fair / Easter*, *Public Holiday*, *Health and Fitness Conference*, *US Book Fair*, *Public Holiday*, *Personal Time Off*, *Sales Conference*, *Food Symposium*, *Frankfurt Book Fair*, *Public Holiday*, *Xmas & New Year*.

Figure 2.3 A global schedule form, with external events marked

regular department or committee meetings that you must attend in another colour; they not only occupy a specific period of time but might also be deadlines for completing plans or taking action. Now you can see at a glance which, if any, of the events you have marked overlap; this can influence how you plan the time for your other activities.

You control and can schedule the remainder of the time, including your own holidays. In your publishing plan you decided how you would build the list: what kinds of book you would be publishing, when and in what order. Write down the working titles of the books in your plan. Working backwards from publication dates, estimate the date by which manuscripts must be in-house. Continuing to work backwards, and allowing a suitable amount of time for authors to research, write and revise, as appropriate, you will see the dates by which you must contract them, and that reveals the time within which you have to do your research, find your authors and prepare your proposals. These activities and others, as we discuss below and in Chapter 3, also need to be scheduled to optimize your time and bring your plans to fruition.

At this early stage your schedule is based on estimates and should allow a reasonable amount of contingency time. You will revise it as you work. You might have to alter dates because of advice from your editorial, design and production colleagues. You might add co-editions from other publishers or packaged books, bring forward certain titles to coincide with external events, and push others back because authors need more time to write than you estimated. Every time you revise the schedule you will be able to see the impact that that action has on the other titles and on the plan as a whole.

Developing the idea

Now that you know your list and your company's capabilities, and have established your priorities for development and your schedule, you are ready to start developing your ideas. In fiction publishing, the ideas and approach are usually the authors', and the specification predetermined or very limited in choice. Some nonfiction publishers are design-led, and the editor's job is to fit an editorial treatment of a subject into a predetermined mould, but here we are concerned with the widest range of editorial input, illustrated nonfiction publishing in which you have to find or create ideas (see Chapter 1) and give them form. For each title, consider who the intended audience is (age, interest level, knowledge level, location) and whether the book will cover the whole subject or one aspect, superficially or in depth, with an index or academic apparatus.

Making these decisions, on your own or with the advice of consultants, should help you to give the ideas a physical form. You examined the specifications in researching the list and in outlining your programme, and now you can choose which ones are appropriate to the editorial treatment of each idea. Visualize yourself as the intended reader holding the finished book and turning the pages. Look at the different aspects in your mind's eye, rearranging them until you get a picture that seems to answer all the needs of the book and the reader, then decide:

1   The format
   - trimmed page size
   - landscape or portrait
   - type of binding
2   The extent
   - number of pages
   - number of words
3   The illustrations
   - type(s)
   - total number and proportion of each type
   - number in colour and monochrome
   - inserts, wraps or integrated
   - spatial ratio to text

Keep looking at that book. How much are you, the intended reader, willing to pay for it? Your research of the list and the competition might supply the answer, or you may find it necessary to go out and research the market again, focusing on price and perceived value for this kind of book. What does your research tell you about the optimum print run for this type of book at this price? You may get confirmation of your interpretation or a different view when you talk to the sales manager (see 'Checking sales potential', below).

Author, author

You know what the book is about and who it is aimed at, and you have a vision of what it will look like, so now you need to choose or confirm who is going to write it. Whether projects are offered to you by new or established writers or you have found people who might bring your ideas to life, you have to evaluate the prospective authors as carefully as you do the ideas.

On offer: unpublished writers

Examine submissions for information about the author. The covering letter may be the first indicator of an author's communication skills, and first impressions are important.

- Is it neat, clean and well typed? If the author has not made an effort to make this short document of introduction presentable, how will he or she prepare a longer manuscript?
- Is it clear and concise? Anyone seriously interested in being published should know that commissioning editors are busy people whose attention they need to arrest; if they cannot make a clear point in a letter, what hope is there for a book?
- Does it explain the author's qualifications for writing on this subject? If not, the writer has not thought about what the reader of the letter wants and needs to know; will the same apply to writing the book? If the author has supplied this information but you are not sure of its worth, check with your consultants or advisers.
- Does it indicate who the book is aimed at and why they will want it? The absence of such information might indicate that the writer has not thought about the readers at all, which has implications for the level of information and the level of language in the proposed publication, and for sales and marketing.

Covering letters written by agents should provide the basic information about proposals and authors' qualifications, but they will not reveal as much about the authors as their own letters. The synopsis also offers clues to the author's communication skills, qualifications and awareness of the readers' needs.

- Is it neat, clean and well typed?
- Does it provide enough detail to make the scope and content of the book as a whole and of each chapter clear?
- Is the material organized logically?
- Is there anything obvious missing?
- Does it include anything obviously or apparently irrelevant?

Synopses that are less than perfect in any of these areas are not necessarily grounds for rejecting authors but can indicate the kind of support they might need. The sample chapter reveals more.

- Does it deliver the content promised in the synopsis?
- Is the level of information and language appropriate to the intended audience?
- Is the information conveyed in an interesting way?
- Is the writing coherent and grammatical?
- Is the spelling correct and consistent?

When you do not know the answers, pass the material to someone who does: an adviser, a consultant, a copy-editor. Even when you think you know all the answers, it might be wise to have them confirmed by others.

Nor all that glisters: established authors

There are two kinds of established author: those you have worked with before and those you have not. The first kind seem like a gift: you know what they are qualified to do and how they perform ... or do you? Let us assume that if they are proposing to write on a different topic or for a different audience from before, you will scrutinize their ability to do so as you would any new author's, just as you will examine the saleability of the proposed book itself. What else you do depends on the extent of your involvement with the author following the signing of the previous contract and delivery of that manuscript. You should know whether the author delivered the manuscript and any other materials on time and whether these conformed to the synopsis or subsequently agreed brief. However, you might have to read the file or talk to the managing editor or copy-editor to find out whether

- the amount of revision and/or editing of the text or ancillary materials was consistent with original expectation,
- the author was cooperative and helpful in responding to queries and suggested alterations to text and illustrations,
- the author read and returned proofs on schedule.

You should also be able to get some feedback about the author from sales and marketing when you consult your colleagues about the proposal (see 'Checking sales potential', below). Once again, what you learn will not necessarily cause you to reject an author, but it can prepare you and your colleagues better for working with him or her.

Authors you have not worked with also fall into two groups: those published by your company and those published elsewhere. You can read the file on the authors you have inherited in-house and discuss them with colleagues, as described above. You might get additional information from the previous commissioning editors, even if they have moved to other firms, if you know where they are.

Authors might come to you from other firms because you publish for a different market. However, if this is not the case, happy as you may be to add them to your list, ask them why they have left their previous publisher: were they unhappy with the way they or their books were treated, or did the company turn down their next proposal? Do you know the relevant commissioning editors at the other firms? It is not uncommon and it is useful for editors working in the same field to know each other. Perhaps you have heard about authors while they were working for another firm; perhaps you will make discreet inquiries now. Remember, you cannot always judge authors by their books alone.

An idea in search of an author

As with so many tasks in publishing, there is no single way of approaching someone to write a book. It can be that you have an idea and have asked advisers or consultants to recommend an author, or have identified promising individuals yourself. In this case you would probably describe the book you envisage and discuss your outline of the text, then ask the prospective writers to comment on, revise or flesh out the synopsis, and move on from there to getting a sample chapter. Or you may have met people, let us say at a conference or seminar, and discussed with them writing a book on their specialist subject to fit in with your list. You would probably describe the physical book and ask them to prepare the synopsis and sample material along the lines you have discussed. In both situations you would agree a delivery date for the material, and you would send a letter confirming the brief. Mark that delivery date on your schedule so that you remain aware of it. When the material arrives, you can evaluate these authors as you would anyone who had made an unsolicited submission. In addition, you have the first evidence of their reliability.

- Did they deliver on time? If not, was the delay significant and did they give you any warning?
- Did they follow the brief? If not, did they give sound reasons for their deviation?

This is also an opportunity to check your communication skills.

- Did you check with them that you were allowing sufficient time for the material to be prepared?
- If you received no warning of the delay, did you contact them to see what the problem was and how long the delay would be?
- Was the brief absolutely clear and unambiguous?

Remember, the information you obtain can help you to improve your communication and management skills and your working relationships.

It is essential to give your potential authors feedback soon after receiving their material. Do not leave them in the void wondering what is happening — they might lose confidence or interest in the project or in working with you. And do not wait for them to contact you; they might not, but if they do and you can give them the information then, they will wonder why you did not take the initiative. Any way you look at it, you lose. Be a winner: keep your authors informed. It takes very little time and it can do as much, or more, for your relationship than taking them to lunch.

Acknowledge that you have received and read their contribution and explain to all authors, not just novices, what you want them to do or what you will do next:

- you would like them to revise particular points along certain lines, or
- you will send it out for consultants' reports, or
- you have made some minor adjustments, or
- you will discuss it with your colleagues, who might recommend changes before you prepare the formal proposal.

Let your authors know when you plan to have further information for them, ideally in a number of weeks, and mark that time on your schedule as a deadline for contacting them. Of course, you might contact them sooner; for example, if you want to send them a consultant's report or discuss alterations suggested by your colleagues. Despite your best efforts, schedules are not always kept, so as soon as you know that there will be a delay, for whatever reason, tell your authors.

Checking sales potential

Having reached this stage with a number of ideas, you can complete estimate requests and send them to production (see Chapter 8), and get estimates of other costs from design and copy-editing (see 'Editorial and design time and money', below). If the proposals are for tried and tested products, books made to a well-known formula, the estimates should confirm what you already know about costs and margins. For books that differ in any significant aspect, the estimates provide the information you need to see if the project will achieve an acceptable margin. However, you might decide that you need to confirm the saleability of the book before you start number crunching.

In either case, it is time to sound out your good colleague in sales. You want the sales manager's full attention and considered opinion on your estimated prices and print runs. If you are planning to include any income from subsidiary rights, you will need to repeat the process with the rights manager (see also 'Planning co-editions', below). It could be that your colleagues support your ideas and agree with your opinion of sales potential. Thus two short meetings can leave you confident about your plans and assured of support for the proposals.

Of course, either or both the sales and rights managers could disagree with your view of sales potential. When this happens, some people spend time and energy in defending their ideas, often by simply denying the validity of the objections. This is a common human reaction, particularly among creative people who see their ideas as an extension of themselves. Here is some advice: do not fall into the trap of treating every opposing view as a personal attack. Focus on the real object of the criticism, which is not you but some aspect of a particular book or books. Do not waste time reiterating why you think you are right; invest it finding out exactly why your colleagues think the estimates of sales or the prices are wrong and by how much. Do not assume that they are simply lazy, that they want unrealistic bargain prices and short print runs to make selling books easier. Instead, find out where they think the weakness lies: in the idea, the treatment, the author, some aspect of the specification. If the managers have misunderstood or misinterpreted the market you are targeting or the nature of the product, you may be able to clarify these issues — and you will have gained some feedback on how to improve your presentation. If they have understood the proposals perfectly, you will be able to pinpoint the areas you need to reconsider. In either case your colleagues will appreciate that you have consulted them, and so you will have helped to create or maintain good working relationships. Being objective may require a conscious effort, but it makes you more effective at your job.

If you have not already done so, get estimates now. Prepare several requests (see Chapter 8) to cover different print runs and other variations, so that you have all the information you need to review and modify your proposal.

Planning co-editions

Because colour illustrations are expensive to use and reproduce, many illustrated books are dependent on co-edition deals, which includes book clubs as well as foreign publishers. The nonoriginating publishers contribute to the cost of creating the book, and printing together produces economies in material and manufacturing costs. International co-editions must appeal to readers in a number of countries and not seem foreign to any of them. Some subjects lend themselves to this treatment more easily than others. However, it is not enough for you to propose books on suitable subjects and get the rights manager's agreement; you have to understand what makes books work as international co-editions because you will be briefing the authors. The dangers are that, in trying to make such a co-edition, lists of examples or nuggets of material relevant to each of the participating countries are added to the text like a patchwork quilt, making most of the book uninteresting to most of the readers, or any information that might seem foreign to any country is omitted, leading to a boring book devoid of character. There are pitfalls to be avoided for each subject and each country. If you do not have the experience of what these are and how to avoid them by the time you are responsible for commissioning co-editions, ask your colleagues — other commissioning editors, copy-editors, rights personnel — for help.

Editorial and design time and money

As well as getting manufacturing costs from production, you also need to get figures, or check the ones you are using, for the editorial and design components. It is possible that you have extensive, up-to-date knowledge for all the costs you need. None the less, it is better to discuss the parts of the proposal that will affect other people with them: perhaps you have overlooked something; perhaps you are not as up-to-date as you think; perhaps you have misunderstood or misinterpreted information; perhaps there is another way of doing something that you have not considered — we do not know what we do not know until we ask or someone tells us, and colleagues are unlikely to tell us until we give them an opportunity to do so.

Let us assume that in your firm some of the books are edited and designed in-house and some are freelanced, and there is a managing editor and a design manager who make these decisions. Outline the proposed project to them and ask if there is an inherent aspect that will determine which way the book will be handled. Get estimates for any of the work that will or *might* be freelanced; Figure 2.4 shows the usual editorial and design fixed costs — the ones incurred regardless of the size of the print run. *Discuss* what you want and what they say until you are sure you understand not only what the rate for each job is, but what quality or quantity of work that rate buys. For example, is the editing rate for:

- imposing basic house style, spelling and consistency, or will it cover more intensive work on content, language and structure?
- working on hard copy only or also putting editorial changes onto disk?
- working on the text only or also editing captions, preparing briefs for artwork, and cutting and filling at page?
- collating the author's and proofreader's proofs?

Similarly, is the proofreading rate for one, two or more stages of proofs?

Whether a book is being prepared on disk and corrected on a desktop publishing (DTP) system by editors and designers or being typeset conventionally will influence the estimate of production costs and the schedule, and can influence the way you plan the work and brief the author. It might even influence which author you choose.

When the designer knows what effect you want, she or he might be able to advise you on a number of ways of achieving it that have different cost and quality implications. When the designer knows what market you are trying to reach, he or she may be able to contribute fresh visual ideas that will give your project more appeal.

Editorial costs	
Translation	
Copy-editing	
Proofreading	
Indexing	
Text permissions	
Consultants	
Other editorial	
Picture researcher	
Picture fees	
Total	

Design costs	
Book design	
Layouts	
Artwork	
Photography	
Jacket design	
Total	

Figure 2.4 Typical editorial and design fixed costs

Discuss the schedules in general now too. You need to know whether the publication dates you are planning are realistic. Only if your colleagues say they are not do you need to discuss the schedules in any detail, so that you can see where the problems lie and work together to overcome them. Depending on your experience, you may not yet know enough about the editorial, design and production processes to judge schedules adequately. Use this and other similar opportunities to become better informed.

Being an effective communicator means listening as well as talking; inviting and considering other people's ideas as well as explaining your own. Teamwork on a project begins when you involve your colleagues, and the earlier you do so, the more help you will have in getting the job done well.

Look at it another way

Revising your proposal may not be the most fun you have ever had, but the more positively you approach it, the easier it will be. Forget how much time and effort you have put into creating the proposal. Consider it as objectively as possible, as if you are seeing it for the first time, with the benefit of your colleagues' comments. Look first at the objections that have been voiced and then try to find ways to overcome them. Here are a few starting points, each of which can apply to the domestic and foreign markets (see also 'Planning co-editions', above).

- If the idea is weak, how can you strengthen it? Is it too specialized to appeal to a wide market or too general to appeal to a discerning one? Is it seasonally sensitive? Is the treatment too broad or too narrow? Too radical or clichéd?
- If the problem is that the proposed author is not well known in this field, can you get someone who is to write a foreword? (Your preparation should ensure that you have the right author: see 'Author, author', above.)
- If the proposed price is too high, you know that you cannot simply increase the print run, so you have to consider whether you can improve the specification to justify the price without increasing the costs, or reduce the price by cutting the costs without noticeably diminishing the value.
- If the proposed print run is too high, you know that you cannot simply increase the price. Again, you have to see if you can cut the costs without diminishing the perceived value so that you can maintain your margin.

Strengthening the idea

Think about the issues your colleagues have identified, then go back to your authors and consultants and explain the position. As an effective communicator, you know it will save time to focus their attention on the problems in an objective and constructive way: 'My colleagues advise strengthening these points' rather than 'We think the weaknesses in your material are ...' . Since you have thought about these matters, you may have suggestions that you want the authors to comment on, and they may have suggestions that you need to consider; either way, there should be a discussion. The result might be a satisfactory revision of the material or an agreement for the authors to revise the material along agreed lines by a particular date.

Justifying the price

Improving the specification is tempting, and sometimes necessary, but doing so without increasing costs significantly is a hurdle. Making the text longer will not increase author costs if the author is on a royalty and will not add dramatically to the typesetting bill. Depending on how many words are involved, it might have a negligible effect on freelance copy-editing and proofreading costs, if these service are to be used. This can be a useful tactic if the purpose of the extra words is to provide a wider or deeper coverage of the subject. However, if the purpose of the extra words is to increase the extent, you know that the proportionately high cost of paper could cancel out this benefit. The number of pages might not be as important to the customer as the size of the book; if you think this is the case, talk to production about the possibility of increasing the bulk.

Increasing the number of illustrations is a tempting way to justify the price, but it will cost more in permissions for photographs or illustrators' fees for artwork and in origination fees. The same is true of maintaining the number of illustrations but increasing their size on the page, or having more illustrations in colour rather than black and white. Talk to your team to see if there is a trade-off here: can the book achieve better visual impact with fewer but larger illustrations in colour and, if so, can this be done without increasing costs?

Cutting the spec

Bringing down the price while maintaining the margin means looking at the same issues as above but from a different angle. For example, cutting the text will not reduce author costs if the author is on a royalty, nor reduce the typesetting bill dramatically, and is likely to have a negligible effect on freelance copy-editing and proofreading costs, if these service are to be used. And there is no point doing it in order to save on paper, because cutting the extent will result in a lower perceived value.

Perhaps the illustrative element can be manipulated. Is the planned number of illustrations critical or is there some scope for reducing it without affecting the perceived value? Decreasing the number of illustrations will save on permissions or illustrators' fees and on origination. Reducing the number that are in colour would result in only marginal savings on permissions fees, but would save on origination and could have a greater impact on costs if it meant the book could be printed 4/1 or 4/2 instead of full colour throughout.

Talk to the editorial and design managers again. You can approach costs from two points of view: (1) how, and how much, can they be reduced without a noticeably detrimental effect on value or (2) what will be the effect of cutting them by a specific amount? Perhaps part or all of the editorial work can be done in-house rather than freelance, or certain design elements can be modified to save money; perhaps a lower budget will mean restricting the proportion of photographs that come from certain sources or limiting the choice of illustrator; or perhaps it will mean harder negotiating with suppliers generally.

There is no point in trying to impose a much lower budget while insisting on the same level of quality; in the end you get what you pay for. It is also dangerous to pare down a budget to cover minimal essential costs. A sound budget has a small contingency allowance; if you remove it to make your figures look better, you also remove the safety net that prevents you from going over-budget or compromising on quality if anything unexpected happens.

Acceptance

You have done your research, consulted your colleagues, reviewed and revised your ideas and crunched your numbers until you feel sure the proposals are strong. If your company does not insist on written proposals, prepare notes to support your presentation; they will also be useful for preparing promotional materials later (see Chapter 11). It will, of course, be disappointing if any of your proposals are not accepted, but you are experienced enough to look at the problem objectively, find out what the stumbling blocks are and take action to overcome them. Occasionally, you will find that it is better to start from the beginning than to try to revamp an already reworked idea.

When proposals are accepted, the company makes a commitment to time as well as money. The publication dates set now signal the moments at which the company expects to see the beginning of returns on its investments. To fulfil these expectations, you have agreed the overall timescales with your editorial, design and production colleagues and now you have to ensure that the projects are available for them to work on at the agreed time. How accurate and reliable the estimates of time and money prove to be depends on how accurate the initial information is and how everyone involved does their job. How well you do your job influences how well others will be able to do theirs, and, therefore, how good the entire job will be.

3

From proposal to manuscript

During the preparation of the proposal you and the authors discussed the subject, approach, target readership, number of words, and number and type of illustrations, and maybe even the design of the book. Because you are an effective editor and have kept your authors informed of progress, they are enthusiastic and ready to commit themselves to the project. This is a very positive atmosphere in which to brief them on delivering the manuscript and to negotiate the contract. Maintain it by preparing yourself: plan an agenda. Bearing in mind that the best briefings are *brief,* review your information, check that you understand all points yourself and have available any materials — house style guide for authors, specimen pages, previous books in the series — that you want to give the authors. Also consider whether it would be beneficial to include other members of the team — copy-editor and designer, for example — in all or part of the meeting.

The brief

Start the briefing by reviewing the project details mentioned above, particularly if any of them have changed as a result of the approval meeting. Explain to new authors, and remind experienced ones of, the processes the manuscript will go through on its way to becoming a book, and what they are expected to do and who will be in contact with them at each stage. This is your first opportunity to emphasize how important it is for the success of the project that the authors follow the brief, deliver on time and in the agreed manner, and make only essential changes at proof stage. Make sure that they understand not only the words you use but also the meaning. Often it is useful to reinforce points by giving examples of what can happen to projects when authors deviate from the brief or the schedule; moan, shake your head sagely, laugh ruefully but get the message home — this is one way in which previous unhappy experiences can be put to a constructive use!

Particularly with authors with whom you are working for the first time and those on long schedules, agree a date by which they will submit the first chapters or drafts of them, and disks if they are preparing their manuscript on computer. Delivery of the draft materials is the first indication of the authors' ability to work to schedule and provides an opportunity for either party to raise and discuss any problems with the content — level, length, structure, illustrations — encountered so far. You can also pass the materials to the copy-editor for comment on the amount of editing that might be needed and to check whether the authors have followed the guidelines for preparing the disks. Your own analysis and the feedback you get may mean that you can be confident that your authors are following the brief or that you need to pull them back on course.

The more authors involved in a single publication, the more helpful it is to have a general editor through whom you communicate with the other contributors and to whom you delegate responsibility for ensuring that they deliver their manuscripts and proofs on time and in the prescribed manner. If there are not more than, say, six contributors, it might be a good idea for them all to attend the initial briefing; but when the number is greater or the contributors are geographically widespread, it will probably not be practical.

The contract

Read the contract thoroughly. Delete clauses that are irrelevant. Add the required details to relevant clauses, identify those with which the authors or their agents might disagree in principle or particulars, and rehearse your negotiating position. Contracts cover many issues in addition to financial terms: be certain that you understand them. Be sure how flexible you can be on all points — take advice from senior or more experienced colleagues where necessary — and have sound reasons for your stance. People will understand and respect that you may have to refer some issues to a higher authority, but they will not be impressed if you are poorly informed, inflexible or unable make a single decision.

The contract is another step in developing your relationship with an author. It is always important to discuss contracts, and it is particularly important to do so in person when working with an author for the first time. Unless the author is more experienced than you, take them through the contract, not reading it word for word but explaining the purpose of each clause and drawing attention to specific details, such as the delivery date, the number of words, the ownership of copyright, who has responsibility for clearing permissions or preparing the index, as well as the financial arrangements for all the various rights. The author might want to negotiate some points immediately; suggest you make a note of each one and then discuss them all over lunch. Then do so.

Going to lunch provides a respite, a temporary and welcome change of focus. Both parties return to the negotiations during the meal more relaxed. It might still be necessary to leave some points to be resolved later. Even when authors are ready to sign, it is a good idea to suggest that they may want to take the contract away and have their legal adviser look at it. In this way you preclude the likelihood of authors later complaining that they did not understand the terms or that the terms are unfair and they have been exploited.

If contracts are directed to agents with whom you have never worked, start building your relationship now. You want to cultivate people who, throughout your career, may be able to bring you new authors and help you work with existing ones. It is useful and appropriate to invite agents to lunch or, if they are too busy, to offer to see them in their office. Face to face, particularly with the support of a pleasant ambience, you can discuss the author, the project and, of course, the contract. An agent's job is to protect and promote an author's interests, the majority of which are enumerated in the contract. Good agents know what terms to expect and will try to improve them where possible. To be respected, you must show that you know what is expected too and have considered and sensible reasons for suggesting anything else.

Discuss how you will work with the authors: when you will brief them and how you will maintain contact while the work is being written. Emphasize the importance of the delivery date and acknowledge the agent's role in ensuring that the authors meet it. Invite cooperation and foster it by keeping agents informed of developments: the authors are theirs as well as yours.

Nurturing authors

After you contract a book, you continue to work on the development of other ideas and might assume that the author is confidently writing. You could be wrong on both points: the author might not be confident and might not be writing.

Home alone

Authors work in isolation. People commissioned to write a work of nonfiction might feel confident about their knowledge of the subject and in their initial enthusiasm be able to produce a synopsis and sample chapter. The deadline is usually short and the motivation great — do it and you might get to write a book — and the idea of a sample is reassuring: it is not the final version. Then comes the inevitable hiatus between submitting sample material and signing the contract. If you keep authors informed of progress during this time and the interval is not too long, they might well retain their enthusiasm; but when the commission is confirmed, they have to produce what they think of as the final manuscript. If the deadline seems far off, even if it is only adequate, some people might delay, or be delayed by other events in their life, and then find they cannot complete on time. Even if they start immediately, they might find writing 'for real' is proving more difficult than providing just a sample. Perhaps, particularly if they are first-time authors, the very idea of writing begins to overwhelm them; they are uncertain how to organize or handle certain information, how much detail to include, how to create tables, diagrams or references. Experienced writers, of fiction or nonfiction, can also encounter difficulties, often described summarily as writers' block. Confidence is pushed aside by frustration and anxiety. Friends, relatives and colleagues may sympathize, but they cannot help.

Staying in touch

You are busy; of course you are. Most authors know, or at least assume, that. True, every now and then there are writers who think theirs is the only book you are publishing, and contact you repeatedly for information, for help, to complain or just to hear your voice. They are the exceptions that prove the rule. The majority do not phone you because they

- do not want to bother such a busy and important person,
- may find it difficult to explain that they are having trouble doing the very thing you have hired them to do,
- do not realize that it is your job to help them.

The first that many editors know of a problem is when the manuscripts do not arrive on schedule or the ones that do arrive are not what they were expecting. Do not join this crowd. You have invested the company's money in producing these books, and your reputation in selecting not only the ideas but also the right authors to develop them; you want to protect both those investments. What you do at this point in your relationship can influence how people develop as writers, how well their present manuscript turns out, and their opinion of you as an individual and as a representative of your publishing house, the last of which may also affect their attitude towards other people in the company with whom they will have to work, from project editors to publicists.

In order to see the books you commissioned come to fruition as you envisaged them, you must stay in touch with them from contract to bound copy, and that means being in contact with authors throughout the writing period. Your job at this stage is to encourage and support all your authors and to find ways to help those who are having difficulties. The very fact that you communicate with them will be encouraging, as it is evidence of your continuing interest in them and in the books. It is your opportunity to give them any relevant company news and to ask them how their work is going and, specifically, if there is anything you can do to help. The help that is needed will depend on the authors and the type of book. It may range from providing reassurance that they are proceeding in a sensible way to suggesting alternative approaches, from sending a useful reference book to supplying the names of possible research assistants or typists. So how can you do this for your many authors while still fulfilling all your other obligations?

Check that schedule

When you sign a contract, put the manuscript delivery date on your schedule (see Chapter 2), no matter how far in the future it is. If you have agreed a date or dates for the submission of draft or early chapters, put them on the schedule too. Now pick a week a reasonable length of time after the contract was signed and mark it on the schedule in a colour or with a symbol used for no other purpose. Some time during that week, telephone the author to offer encouragement and help. Each time you talk with the author you will gain some information about them and the work, and will be able to judge how much time to allow before making contact again. You will want to check back relatively soon with authors who have been having problems to see if they have overcome them, and at longer intervals with the others to make sure no obstacles have appeared in their path. Mark the next contact date on the schedule. Be sure to keep the schedule where you can see it easily and look at it every day. That way you do not have to clutter your mind trying to remember the dates on which or by which you must take action or when you expect manuscripts and reports to arrive: the schedule is your memory.

By taking care of your authors in this way throughout the gestation period, you nurture their development as writers as well as your relationship. You also have repeated opportunities to guide authors in revising their manuscripts in order to make them acceptable. Sorting out problems as they arise minimizes the risk of unpleasant surprises in the final manuscripts and of unexpected delays, and maximizes the progress of the books on schedule and in line with your brief. You are in control. And you want to stay there.

Assessing manuscripts

Did you know that there are editors who do not read the manuscripts they have commissioned? They usually claim they do not have enough time, that the copyeditor will do it, or that they know the author's work and this manuscript, like previous ones, will be fine. Do not be seduced by such reasons; in reality, they are very poor excuses.

Making time

Schedules are one of the driving forces of publishing. To be effective, you must control them, not let them constrain you. You began taking control when you created an annual schedule of your publishing programme (see Chapter 2). You increased that control by using the schedule to trigger contact with your authors, and you will extend it by allocating time to assessing manuscripts. In the week that a manuscript is due, set aside time to read it. Write it on your schedule as you would any important meeting; in this case it is a very private meeting, just you and the text. Like other meetings, of course, you want to arrange not to be disturbed, and you know that if you find out in advance that the manuscript will be delayed (and you will because you are keeping in touch with the author), you can reschedule the meeting. Before you fall into the trap of claiming that you do not have enough time to do this fundamental part of your job, check how you are spending it. Perhaps there are:

● better ways of organizing your time,
● less important matters that you could delegate,
● meetings that could be shorter or less frequent,
● ways to curtail inessential interruptions,
● personal chores that have been creeping into work time.

Caveat emptor

It is your responsibility as the buyer to check that each author has fulfilled the contract: that the work is complete, conforms to the synopsis and is of acceptable length and quality. You cannot rely on knowing an author's previous work. Each book is unique, and the current manuscript may not be of the same standard as any of his or her earlier ones. If you know the author's work only from its published form, you have no idea how much work the original manuscripts required. If you have read the author's earlier manuscripts, you may find you can read this one more quickly than one by an author's whose work is completely unfamiliar, but read it you should. Whether or not it is an author's first book or thirty-first, whether it conforms to the contract in every way or needs revision, you must be in a position to discuss the content with him or her as well as with other members of the publishing team.

If the manuscript is far longer or shorter than stated in the contract, you have to decide whether to publish at the submitted length or return the manuscript to the author to revise. You can make that decision only if you have read the text. If it is shorter than planned, is anything missing or are there any areas that need amplification? If it is longer than planned, are there any areas that can be dropped or easily reduced? If the content would not benefit from lengthening or shortening, you need to work out the cost and price implications of publishing at the submitted length and discuss them with your colleagues. For example:

- Will the book still appeal to the same market?
- Will it have the potential to sell the same number of copies?
- Will the net profit margin still be acceptable?

If you have read drafts of the early chapters, you will now want to check how the author has handled suggested revisions, and you may have an indication of what elements in the text might need particular attention. There could be cost implications if the author has deviated from the original brief in a significant way or failed to make required changes to disks. It may be that structural shortcomings, inconsistencies and minor problems of length can be remedied by the copy-editor, but you are wasting valuable time if you do not assess what action is appropriate and then brief the copy-editor accordingly. There is also the possibility that subtle ways in which the manuscript does not fulfil your expectations will be overlooked and the opportunity for improving the text missed.

Briefing colleagues

The purpose of briefing is to communicate to others the essential information and instructions that will enable them to do their jobs.

What to include

When you are preparing proposals, you give the production department, and perhaps the project editors, in-house picture researchers and designers, the first and most basic briefing: the specifications on which to base their estimates. As mentioned in Chapter 2, you might also provide designers with information about the market and the visual effect you want so that they can advise you on ways of achieving it cost-effectively.

When authors supply draft materials, take this opportunity to send the hard copy and disks to the project editors to check their editability, and to the designers to prepare specimen pages. Colleagues in both departments may provide you with useful feedback for the authors and such work now can save valuable time on the schedule after the manuscript is received. Because you may have had to alter a proposal in a number of ways before it was accepted, the briefing now should include the final specifications (see page 19) as well as the following information.

1 Subject
2 Approach
   - the whole subject or one aspect
   - superficially or in depth
   - with an index or academic apparatus

3 Target reader
  - age
  - interest level
  - knowledge level
4 Market
  - domestic
  - specific foreign countries
  - international co-edition
5 Type of book
  - individual
  - in an existing series
  - first of a series
6 Strengths and weaknesses of the competition

Your instructions should make clear what you want each person to do. For example, should project editors check for general editability or are there specific points of structure or content on which you want feedback? Should they check disks for editorial purposes only or be responsible for getting disks checked by design and production too? If you have not previously discussed the books with the designers, you need to tell them the visual effect that you want, particular features or styles that you have in mind and any that you want to avoid. Include a date by which you want the agreed report and specimen pages, and also the date when the complete manuscript is due.

Assessing manuscripts provides you with the final material for briefing your colleagues. If there were no draft materials, the briefs need to include the information outlined above. Even if they were involved earlier, editors and designers will need to be updated and given additional information about the project now. First, notify them of any changes that have been made to the specification; production should be informed of these before they are finalized in case there are technical or cost implications. Then give them or remind them of any information about the authors and the project that will affect their work. For example, have there been any problems with the authors on this or previous books or any agreements on how specific parts of the current manuscript will be treated, are the authors visually unimaginative, and are there any special arrangements or conditions for contacting the authors? Finally, provide feedback on editorial and design work done at the draft stage and indicate what needs to be done now. The main points to include are whether:

- the submission is complete; if it is not, be sure to state when any missing material is expected,
- the text needs to be cut or extended and by how much,

- there are structural or content problems,
- the authors are responsible for clearing copyright permissions and providing the index,
- you know or the editor needs to check that the authors made the necessary changes to the disk;
- changes are needed to the basic design because of developments in the manuscript during writing.

How to do it

A good brief is brief. It contains all the information necessary to produce the results you want, and not so much that it inhibits or restricts the input of others or wastes their time. A handover form is an efficient basis for a brief. It can include the specification, the proposed publication date and price, the materials being handed over and those to come, and the names of all the people involved (see Figure 3.1). It might include space for your instructions to the project editor and designer, or these can be covered in a separate memo. The handover form can remain attached to the manuscript throughout its progress, with the project editor adding information for use by the copy-editor, and the copy-editor adding information for use by the designer. It can also incorporate the designer's type specification, although many companies prefer to make this a separate form.

If you are briefing project editors, designers and production controllers on a book in a series in which you have all been involved, you might find that the information on the form is sufficient. However, if you and your colleagues have not worked together before or the book is significantly different from others on which you have collaborated, arrange a handover meeting. Go over the details together, making sure that you are all in agreement about how to proceed. Encourage your colleagues to ask questions now or later, and if you cannot answer any of their questions at the moment, promise to respond by a particular time, and then do so. You may have questions to ask of them too.

Listen to what the rest of the team have to say, particularly when the points they raise are relevant to the schedules and budgets. If you do not understand the claims they make, ask for clarification. If you think the problems they raise are credible, ask them for suggestions for resolving them. This is important not only for getting the current job done well, but also for building your working relationships. You will be learning about your colleagues' strengths and weaknesses, and they will be learning about yours. Being open to the opinions and advice of others offers you the opportunity to learn, to see your projects from other perspectives, and to facilitate strong teamwork.

Handover Form

ISBN _____ Publication date _____

Title _____

Subtitle _____

Author(s)/editor(s) _____

Translator(s)/compiler(s) _____

Format _____ mm, hb/pb Extent _____

Commissioning Editor _____ Copy-editor _____

Designer _____ Picture researcher _____

Indicate below which items are included with the edited text, and which are to come and when. Delete those that are inapplicable.

❏ half-title _____
❏ half-title verso _____
❏ title _____
❏ title verso _____
❏ dedication _____
❏ epigraph _____
❏ contents _____
❏ preface _____
❏ foreword _____
❏ acknowledgements _____
❏ © permissions _____
❏ list of abbreviations _____
❏ list of figures _____
❏ list of illustrations _____
❏ list of maps _____
❏ list of tables _____
❏ other prelim matter? _____
  _____

❏ text: folios _____

❏ appendix(es) _____
  notes
  ❏ footnotes _____
  ❏ end of chapter _____
  ❏ end of text _____
❏ glossary _____
❏ bibliography _____
❏ further reading _____
❏ useful addresses _____
❏ index _____
❏ other endmatter? _____

photos (indicate no.)
  integrated/section
  ❏ halftone _____
  ❏ colour _____

artwork: roughs/finished
(indicate no.)
  ❏ line _____
  ❏ tone _____
  ❏ b&w _____
  ❏ 2-colour _____
  ❏ 3-colour _____
  ❏ 4-colour _____

maps: roughs/finished
(indicate no.) _____

❏ captions _____
❏ annotation lists _____
❏ tables (indicate no.) _____

Disks
No. enclosed _____

Format _____

Software _____

List of files on disk no. ____
  printout _____

Key to codes on disk no. _____
  printout _____

Figure 3.1 An example of a handover form for use by editors and designers: front

Notes for Designer

Editor: *Supply MS folios in general. In the case of numerous headings, extracts, etc., cite the first few instances and point out any anomalies.*

Running heads
(attach list of shortened
headings if necessary)

recto _____

verso _____

none _____

Section/part openers _____

Chapters _____

Subheads

A _____

B _____

C _____

D _____

other _____

Epigraphs _____

Extracts

verse _____

prose _____

drama _____

correspondence _____

Tabular matter _____

Display matter _____

Lists _____

Footnotes _____

Special sorts/symbols _____

Spaces in text _____

Other items _____

_____

Special instructions _____

_____

_____

_____

4

Effective project management

Although the details vary, the principles of project management are the same regardless of the number of projects you manage and whether you work in-house or freelance: assess, schedule, delegate and check the work, and provide feedback. How well you perform these tasks will affect your ability to fulfil your responsibilities for controlling schedules and budgets, and producing books of the required quality. It will also affect how well others are able to do their job. You must be well organized, have a sound understanding of the processes with which you are dealing, and be an effective communicator.

Styles of management

The style of management you choose for projects depends on the number of projects you are handling, the amount of time you have and the resources available. You might be leading a team on a single extensive and complex title or one with many parts, or be responsible for managing several simple illustrated books simultaneously. You might employ one style for some projects and a different one for others, depending on the nature of the project and the degree of involvement you want or can afford to have.

Assuming that you are not doing the copy-editing yourself (if you are, please read Chapter 5), your main responsibilities will be for coordinating the work of others. You can delegate each aspect of the job — editing, proofreading, picture research, indexing — individually, checking the work at each stage, and liaising with colleagues in other departments. Some project managers even insist on dealing with the author over queries and collating the proofs themselves. This gives them tight control of the project but is not really an efficient use of their time. Because they do not know the text as well as the copy-editor, it takes them time to understand the queries, and longer to deal with the answers and decide which authorial alterations to allow on the proofs. You could pass these responsibilities to the copy-editor and retain your contact with the author in the other stages.

You can reduce your involvement further, and save more time, by deciding who will do each of the editorial tasks but giving the responsibility for briefing and liaising with them to the copy-editor. You can continue to check the work at each stage and either liaise with design and production or also delegate these tasks to the copy-editor while you adopt a supervisory role, thus maintaining control of budgets, schedules and quality. You can still stay in touch with authors, and make it clear to them that you are always available if needed.

Assessing the project

Your first encounter with a project can be as early as the development stage if you work closely with a commissioning editor and are invited to advise on preparation and delivery of the manuscript and disks. In this case you will be fully informed about the project and be in a position to work out the details of the schedule. Otherwise, your introduction to the text might be while it is still in development if a commissioning editor provides you with the first chapters, or it might be when the manuscript is 'complete'. Ideally, you will have been informed in advance of what is coming and when, or, in the less than ideal circumstances that prevail throughout much of publishing, something will arrive unheralded.

When something does arrive on your desk, you need to know what it is before you can determine what to do with it. Commissioning editors should provide all the information you need to begin working, but sometimes they do not. At the very least, they should tell you the title of the project. Then you might be able to find out from the proposal and contract in the files:

- the subject and approach,
- the age, reading level and knowledge level of the target audience,
- the intended format, extent, illustrative content, and price.

By comparing the material with the synopsis, if there is one, you can tell whether you have part or all of the project. Ask for any information you need that is not in a brief or in the files; use your initiative and take control of the project at the first opportunity.

Early appraisal

Commissioning editors sometimes highlight particular elements they want you to consider in chapters received in advance of the complete manuscript, but that is not the limit of your job: your analysis should be thorough. You can use some of the knowledge you acquire to provide advice on what the author needs to do or not do to make the manuscript acceptable, and the rest to help you plan how to handle it when it is complete. Start by looking at the schedule and the proportion of the project that you have. Does it seem likely that the author will

● have time to utilize any feedback in completing the work?
● be able to complete the work by the delivery date?

You will, of course, need to discuss the implications of negative answers to these questions with the commissioning editor.

Next, evaluate the quality and editability of the text in front of you.

● Is it interesting? If not, is it because of the quality of the information or the writing?
● Is the structure clear and sensible?
● Is the information accurate, consistent, logically organized, and explained clearly and in sufficient detail for the intended level of readership?
● Are the language level and tone appropriate to the intended level of readership?
● Are the grammar, punctuation and spelling accurate and consistent?
● Is the use of material from other sources apposite and acknowledged in the appropriate way?
● Are any elements that were expected missing, or any present that were not expected?

Remember, you are not editing, but analysing; not changing the detail, but citing examples. Thus you might point out:

● the types of place where the text would benefit from more or less explanation,
● the need for more or fewer levels of heading,
● that sources need to be acknowledged and, where appropriate, copyright permission sought, and how and when to do this, or state what information the copyeditor will need in order to clear permissions for the author,
● which elements are missing or are unexpectedly present.

If the quality of information or writing is poor, discuss it with the commissioning editor. Perhaps it is no worse than expected or you can suggest ways that the author can improve it. If your combined opinion is that the author is not going to be able to do any better on these or other editorial issues, you know the level of editing that the complete manuscript will require and that it probably will not be economical to use the author's disks for setting, which might mean changing the planned production route and revising estimates and schedules. The author may simply need to be reminded to supply missing elements, but if the unexpected additional material is essential, the commissioning editor will need to check whether it will affect the specification or cost.

Now consider what else this instalment might indicate about the whole. For example:

- Is the material so extensive or so concise that it seems unlikely that the author will be able to meet the contractual length?
- Does the text deliver what was promised in the synopsis?
- Is the number of tables, figures or other illustrations reasonable in relation to the total number allowed?
- Is the hard copy well presented: double spaced, with adequate margins, and minimal, neat and legible handwritten alterations?
- Does the disk match the hard copy, has it been prepared according to agreed guidelines and is it compatible with the systems with which it is intended to be used?

These too are issues that you should discuss with the commissioning editor, as they could all have considerable impact on the schedule, the budget, and the work you and your colleagues in design and production will have to do.

Full-term delivery

Ideally, the commissioning editor will read the completed manuscript before passing it to you, check the length and indicate any important issues for the copy-editor's attention. But, as we all know, we live in a far from ideal world. At least if this is your second encounter with the project, you can check whether the author has implemented the suggestions made in the first assessment or whether those points must now be dealt with in the copy-editing. If this is the first time you have seen the manuscript, you need to evaluate it as explained above to facilitate the editing if you are working on the manuscript yourself or to help you choose an appropriate copy-editor and prepare a brief.

In addition, now that the author has delivered the whole manuscript, you need to consider the following factors.

- *Completeness* Check the synopsis or contract to help you determine whether all the project material has been delivered: full text, illustrations or illustration lists and references, acknowledgements and permissions information, relevant end-matter and ancillary matter. Find out when any missing material is expected.
- *Complexity* The sample or early chapters may not have reflected all the structural elements. Look at the number of levels of heading; the number and variety of types of illustrations; the nature of tables, notes and references; the type and amount of cross-referencing; the amount and types of quotations and other display material.
- *Presentation* Check the extent to which the final text complies with the guidelines for presentation of hard copy and disks, including pagination and file management on disks.

- *Length* Do a quick cast-off (see pages 62–3). Discuss an excessively under- or over-length text with the commissioning editor. Unless he or she decides to accept this deviation from the contract and specification, the manuscript should be returned to the author for revision before copy-editing begins.

Scheduling

Schedules are a constant factor in everything you do, and maintaining them is critical to the success of the project. Most publishing schedules are vertical and record a manuscript's progress through the publishing stages in the most basic way: dates on which materials are transmitted from department to department (Figures 4.1, 4.2). This is a macroscopic critical path analysis of the entire process (see Figure 8.1), showing all the participants when and for how long they will be involved in a project. To be a useful project management tool, the schedule must show the time allocated to the different aspects of the editorial job, not all of which are consecutive. A horizontal format enables you to schedule all your jobs in detail. It can be used not only to tell you when to expect and send materials, and inform people in advance when to expect them, but also to remind you to keep in touch with the other team members.

Create an annual schedule like the one described on pages 16–18. Just as there, highlight public holidays in one colour, and other events that can affect your work but whose dates are outside your control in another. Use a third highlighter to indicate your own holidays; it is just as important to consider your personal time off as it is those other events in planning your projects.

Write the first project title in the left-hand column. You might find it helpful to jot down under it the format, extent and number of illustrations. On one line mark when the manuscript is due and block out the critical path, the consecutive periods of time the project is in editorial, in design and in production, using distinct colours for each function. Even if you were consulted when the schedule was being planned, you should check it after you have assessed the manuscript to make sure there is still adequate time in which to get the job done to the required standard. Has the impact of all the highlighted periods been foreseen and accommodated? If it has not, or if the realities of the manuscript are significantly different from the assumptions on which the schedule was based, discuss the possible problems and solutions with the copy-editor, the designer and the production controller. Make handover dates on Monday mornings rather than Friday afternoons, unless you know that the next stage of work will be done on the weekend.

Stage	Schedule	Revised	Actual
MS in			
MS to design			
MS to production			
Galleys in			
Galleys, illus. and layouts out			
Colour proofs in			
Colour proofs out			
Pages in			
Pages and index out			
Index proofs in			
Index proofs out			
CRC of text, film of illus. in			
CRC and film out			
Ozalid/blues in			
Ozalid/blues out			
Bound copies			

Figure 4.1 A traditional production schedule for an illustrated book

Stage	Schedule	Revised	Actual
Hard copy and disk in			
Disk and illus to design			
Pages and disk to editor			
Colour originals to production			
Colour proofs in			
Pages, disk and index to design			
Index proofs to editor			
Index proofs to design			
Colour proofs out			
Text film out			
Ozalid/blues in			
Ozalid/blues out			
Bound copies			

Figure 4.2 A DTP production schedule for an illustrated book. In this case the editor is inputting changes to text on disk after editing and at page. The designer scans in the illustrations to produce low-resolution colour images on pages and sends the originals out for reproduction.

When you hand over the manuscript to in-house copy-editors, instruct them to allocate time to the various tasks for which they are responsible (see Chapter 5), and to include a specified amount of time — a few days probably — at the end of each stage for you to check the work and have it revised if necessary. Copy the dates when you will be checking the work onto a separate line on your schedule. (See Chapter 9 for scheduling freelance work.)

Now schedule all remaining tasks. The following are some items that are often omitted from the critical path analysis. If they are not scheduled, they are likely to be forgotten until the last minute and will put pressure on scheduled work.

1 *Cover and/or jacket* Is there a detailed schedule for
   ● the brief to be given,
   ● the blurb to be written, approved, set and proofread,
   ● the design to be approved,
   ● the artwork to be finished, proofed, checked and printed?
2 *Catalogue copy* When does it need to be ready, who will do it and who has to approve it?
3 *Blad* This important co-edition sales tool must usually be prepared not long after the manuscript editing has begun. It involves the copy-editor, picture researcher, illustrator, designer and production controller, and must be well managed if it is not to disrupt the progress of the project. (See also Chapter 11.)
4 *Co-edition coordination* Co-edition partners need galleys of all textual matter and proofs of artwork that has annotation so that they can make their translations, and proofs of the pages to prepare their own text pages. It might be easy to signal when to send what to whom with a special symbol on the schedule.

Look at everything you have scheduled (see Figure 4.3) and check that you have accounted for the impact of the highlighted dates. Now go through the same process with all the other projects you are managing. Look at the schedule vertically and see if you or other members of your team have any conflicts, such as trying to work on the same stage of several projects simultaneously on a short schedule. Inform people in advance about the projects they will be assigned, with the beginning and end dates, so they can tell you if they foresee any problems. When you are warned of or spot a potential conflict, discuss possible solutions with the people involved. Perhaps you need to change or add a team member, revise the timing of particular stages of work on a couple of projects, or delegate some of your responsibility on one to give you more time for another.

Even with all your planning, schedules can be disrupted by events outside your control: an author might become unavailable without warning or a team member

Title and spec — Schedule grid with weekly dates across months

Title and spec	Jan 2 9 16 23 30	Feb 6 13 20 27	Mar 6 13 20 27	Apr 3 10 17 24	May 1 8 15 22 29	June 5 12 19 26	July 3 10 17 24 31	Aug 7 14 21 28	Sept 4 11 18 25	Oct 2 9 16 23 30	Nov 6 13 20 27	Dec 4 11 18 25
Project 1 200 x 165.	← arrange freelancer →		Edit →	Design →	Production →	Galley Layout	Production Pages	Production	Film			Books
416 pp. 250 illus	picture researcher					Find indexer →						
Project 2 200 x 165.	← arrange picture researcher →		Edit →	Design →	Production →	Galley Design	Production Pages	Production	Film			Books
256 pp. 500 illus						Find indexer →						
Project 3 185 x 185.				Edit →	Design →	Design →	Design	Production Film		Books		
96 pp. 100 illus. DTP												

Bottom event row (calligraphic labels): New Year · Sales Conference · Bologna Book Fair · Public Holiday · Easter and Easter Conference · US Book Fair · Public Holiday · Personal Time Off · Sales Symposium · Frankfurt Book Fair · Public Holiday · Xmas & New Year

Figure 4.3 A project manager's global schedule

change jobs, a computer could break down or the marketing department might want to accelerate the schedule because a competitor has announced a rival book. Everyone on a project must be made aware that they have a responsibility to inform you at the first sign of a deviation from the agreed timetable, especially a potential delay. When your projects are scheduled in detail and under control, it is easier to cope with the unexpected. The global scheduling form enables you to see the impact of the change on a particular project and on all the others, and therefore helps you, in consultation with your colleagues, to find the best way to handle it. However, to provide this benefit, the form must be where you can see it easily all the time.

Delegating

Choosing copy-editors and proofreaders

Taking care to choose the most appropriate people for your team is the first step in good delegation. Everyone you use should be competent in the basic skills of their discipline, but noone excels at every aspect of the work, and part of your job is to balance an individual's strengths and weaknesses with the requirements of the project. The ability of in-house staff to produce the requisite quality of work on schedule helps you to maintain your budget. If you are using freelancers, you must balance the quality you need with the time available and the price you can pay (see Chapter 9).

Consider the copy-editor. The most basic question is whether you need a subject specialist. Following that decision, look at your project assessment and decide what that person has to be particularly good at; for example:

- checking and styling tables, notes and references,
- handling complex structures,
- restructuring or rewriting,
- cutting or expanding text,
- making sensitive style improvements,
- editing up or down to a particular language level,
- imaginative artwork and illustration briefing,
- handling authors' disks.

Of course you want a good communicator, a person who will be able to deal effectively with the author, you and other team members. Remember to look at your schedule too, and select someone who can deliver the quality of work you need in the time available.

Proofreaders can be subject specialists too, and while anyone you use should be able to pick up typesetting and editorial errors, some are better than others at particular aspects of the job; for example:

- pointing out or resolving inconsistencies,
- correcting bad word breaks,
- raising sensible queries and suggesting possible answers,
- tidying up widows and orphans,
- checking consistency of spacing between elements on pages.

As always, some people produce high quality work at speed, others do so slowly, and some offer speed at the expense of quality. What do you need?

Choosing and briefing indexers is dealt with in Chapter 5, choosing and briefing designers in Chapter 6, and choosing and briefing picture researchers in Chapter 7.

Preparing the brief

Remember, a good brief is brief. It contains all the information other people need to produce the results you want, and not so much that it wastes their time or inhibits or restricts their own contribution. Perhaps the commissioning editor has held a handover meeting or sent you the project with a handover form (see Figure 3.1) and briefing notes. If not, gather the basic information about the project — the technical specification and the editorial points discussed on pages 37–9 — and fill in the relevant parts of the handover form. This should always remain with the manuscript, being updated as necessary as it passes from hand to hand so that each member of the team knows exactly what he or she is receiving, and what material is outstanding and when it is expected.

Base the rest of the brief on the other information and the results of your assessment, and include other appropriate materials, so that you provide the copy-editor with the following information.

1 The relevant background on the:
    - series: copies of other titles to help the editor solve style questions,
    - title: changes already agreed or refused, main problems with the text, importance of the title to the list, specimen pages,
    - author: sensitivities, availability, how to contact,
    - target readership: age, interest level, market.
2 The level of the copy-editing task:
    - minimal: imposing house style, dealing with inconsistencies and infelicities, mark-up for design,
    - medial: as above, plus limited restructuring, rewriting, cutting or expanding,
    - major: as minimal, plus extensive restructuring, rewriting, cutting or expanding.
3 A list of other responsibilities, such as:
    - preparing artwork or other illustration briefs,
    - inputting editorial changes on disk,

- formatting output of disk to be compatible with production route (see Chapter 8),
- tagging and coding disks,
- briefing and liaising with proofreaders, picture researchers and indexers,
- collating proofs.

4 The schedule.

Inexperienced copy-editors who are still working under your close supervision may need to be reminded of the most basic tasks, such as:

- numbering the manuscript consecutively throughout,
- keying in tables and illustrations,
- separating text, tables, notes and captions,
- ensuring all figure annotations are typed.

In the course of their work copy-editors might raise questions that you could not have foreseen when you prepared the brief. Take time to give a considered response so that you do not make more work for the copy-editor or yourself, and risk introducing inconsistencies to the manuscript, by changing your mind later.

Depending on the style of management you have chosen, it may be you or the copy-editor who briefs the proofreader. The handover form is still attached to the manuscript, providing basic information. It may even include the copy-editor's style sheet and the design specification; otherwise, these need to be added to the brief with the schedule. The brief also needs to state the scope of the proofreader's job:

- proofreading against copy or blind,
- listing queries separately as well as on the proof,
- keying in illustrations on galley,
- drawing attention to page references on galley or filling them in on page.

Inexperienced proofreaders working under close supervision may need to be reminded of such basic tasks as using the appropriate colour for marking typesetter and house errors, checking running heads and folios on pages, and checking the numbering of notes and figures.

Arrange handover meetings with individuals or with the entire team, as appropriate, and follow the same procedures as recommended in Chapter 3 ('How to do it', page 39). Be sure to invite all the members of the team to ask for clarification or more information after they have had time to read and absorb the brief.

Checking

It is important to inspect work that you have delegated to ensure that is done to the appropriate standard. The amount of time you devote to this will depend on a number of factors:

● the number of projects you are managing,
● the style of management you have chosen,
● the complexity of the project,
● the relative experience of the various team members and how well you know their work,
● your own level of experience,
● the intended quality of the project.

For example, if other team members are relatively inexperienced or are people with whom you have never worked before, you might check what they have done at every stage; otherwise you might make the copy-editor responsible for checking some of the work — such as the proofreading at galley and page — and reporting to you. On a very large project, the copy-editing might take many weeks or even months to complete, in which case you could check the work early in the process, ask the copy-editor for interim reports and then check the whole job at the end. If the work is being done in batches to save time overall, you might check each batch at every stage or feel confident after two batches that you do not need to check them all. If the title is very important to the list, you are more likely to spend more time verifying its quality than if it is of minor significance. Every project can be different, so be sure to use the global scheduling form to remind you when to check the work on each one.

Like assessment, checking involves analysing the work, not doing it yourself. Bear in mind that no two people work exactly the same way or make the same editorial or design choices, and there can be many equally effective solutions to a problem. The question to ask when checking someone else's work is not 'Is that what I would have done?' but 'Does that make the message clear to the reader?' Depending on the stage of work you are checking, the reader can be anyone involved in the process as well as the target audience for the finished book. Only when the answer to that question is no do you need to intervene.

Copy-editing

Before you look at the work, look at the brief to remind yourself what you asked the copy-editor to do. Then see how specific points have been handled. For example:

- Does the level of rewriting, restructuring, cutting or extending conform to the brief?
- Does the rewriting maintain the author's level and tone of language?
- Are changes or additions to the text appropriate?

Spot check for clarity, accuracy and consistency:
- heading structure,
- application of house style, particularly in references,
- tables and figures,
- first paragraphs, boxes, extracts and other special textual elements.

Check how well the administrative aspects of the work have been done:
- Are the writing, marks and instructions clear?
- Has the handover form been properly updated, and any other requested report or material (such as permissions, artwork and design briefs, prelims) been supplied?
- If the job is being done on disk, is it accompanied by a marked-up hard copy or printout of the edited version?

Proofreading

Remember to look at the brief first so that you can check that the proofreader has fulfilled it. Then *spot check* the proofs to see what they tell you, primarily about the proofreading but also about the copy-editing.

- How heavily marked are the proofs and in what colour? Consider whether the marks reveal editorial inconsistencies or unclear mark-up, or poor keyboarding or typesetting.
- Are the marks used correctly and clearly?
- How many queries have been raised, how useful or necessary are they, and are they sufficiently concise? Again, decide whether the queries reflect inconsistencies or ambiguities that the copy-editor should have resolved.
- Have figures been keyed in and page references marked for attention or filled in as required?

Check whether the proofreader missed anything — typographical errors, omitted or repeated words, bad word breaks, spacing problems — by reading some short passages at random and by comparing the proofs with the author's set.

If you inspect the proofs after they have been collated, check that the decisions that have been made about accepting the author's changes conform to the brief. For example, are only essential corrections allowed or is the author so important that a number of unnecessary changes are acceptable?

Putting it right

Before you start altering what someone else has or has not done, think about the nature and the amount of work involved and, of course, the schedule.

- Is the change absolutely necessary?
- Is the change limited or will it affect the consistency?
- Does the change have to be marked throughout the manuscript or proof, or can it be a general instruction to the typesetter?
- Is there enough time in the schedule for the copy-editor or proofreader to make the corrections or can you do it more efficiently in the time you have available?

Although you might decide to make the changes yourself, you should still include the fact that they needed to be made in the feedback to the original worker.

Providing feedback

Effective editors are not members of that group of people who claim that they do not have time to provide feedback, as if it were not a vital part of their job and therefore something they must make time to do. Everybody can benefit from feedback, not just the people who report to you but all the people with whom you work, including the author and the commissioning editor. Positive feedback boosts confidence and morale, while its absence erodes them; constructive criticism can help people to improve, but its lack can mislead people into thinking that their work is satisfactory although not valued. Either way, not providing feedback is an abdication of responsibility. (See also Chapter 9.)

The best time to give feedback is soon after you have checked another person's work, when it is fresh in both your minds. It is simple to acknowledge a satisfactory job with a general 'Well done', but even more rewarding to point out specific aspects: 'Well done — you've really improved the structure/the tables/the layout' and so on. The message is not only that the work is appreciated, but also that these elements are particularly important. It is especially useful to make such comments if they reinforce a point that you have made previously. 'Thanks for those briefing notes; they really saved a lot of time' reminds the commissioning editor how crucial it is to provide these. To be effective, comments should be sincere and not patronizing.

Many people do not want to give negative feedback because they are afraid of hurting other people's feelings. Be sensitive, be constructive and you can avoid this pitfall. Since your aim is to help people to improve the quality of their work, you have to tell them in what areas they need to do so, and perhaps give them advice on how to go about it.

First, look at the work and at the brief. Then, trying to be as objective as possible, consider to what extent the shortcomings lie in the performance and to what extent in the brief. This can be useful feedback for *you*, helping you to see how you can improve your delegating and briefing techniques. For example, do the deficiencies in the work indicate that the individual lacked the right skills or experience? Perhaps you need to be more careful in selecting the most appropriate person or, if your choice is limited by circumstance, you need to compensate for perceived limitations by providing closer supervision and more support. It is also possible that you chose someone for their known strengths and this is the first indication of their weaknesses; you can bear that in mind when you delegate another job. Was some aspect of the job not handled in the way you wanted? Maybe you need to make the brief more explicit, make the language clearer or check that everyone has the same understanding of the desired outcome before the work begins. Such self-awareness is a useful perspective when you are evaluating the work of others.

Balance the feedback: commend the good aspects first and then point out what was not done or what was not done to the expected standard. Remember to objectify the comments, to focus on the work rather than the person. It is easier for people to accept 'this needs to be done like this/more clearly/consistently' and so on than 'you didn't/don't/should have …'. Be honest: admit if the brief was inadequate or ambiguous. Remind your colleagues, too, always to ask you for clarification or additional information if they need it. Conclude with a positive statement so that people are not demoralized but encouraged to heed your advice and do better.

For providing feedback to commissioning editors when they or the authors want to make late or extensive changes to books, see page 76.

Managing editors

When you are delegating the project management of titles, you still have to assess the work to decide who are the most appropriate people to do it, but the level of information in the commissioning editors' briefs will probably be sufficient for that purpose. The main elements you add to the brief for project editors are the parts of the budget for which they are responsible and the schedule. Overseeing projects at arm's length, you provide support where it is needed and can instruct the project editors to report to you at key stages so that you can ensure that quality, budgets and schedules are maintained.

Managing the schedules is vital. By putting the critical path of every project on a global schedule you can see all of the following at a glance:

- how to distribute the work among your resources so that noone is overloaded or underemployed,
- where the key stages are for each title so that you know when to take action, such as checking in advance that manuscripts will arrive on time or that particular people will be available, and when to make time to read reports,
- how a delay or a need to accelerate can affect the project in which it occurs and impact on other projects so that you can take appropriate action.

Budgets

Everyone has a responsibility for the budget, whether they control the amounts paid to others, are themselves listed as a direct cost on a title or are an anonymous drop in the overheads bucket. The last category is where the principle of control begins. Overheads are calculated on the basis that the staff they cover will do a certain amount of work to the required standard within a particular amount of time. If people take longer or do the work to a lower standard, they are increasing the overheads. Taking longer, for example, may mean delayed or fewer publications, or the expense of hiring extra staff to prevent these results. Extra staff mean not only more money on salaries but also increases in the cost of providing space, equipment and facilities. Below-standard performance incurs the cost of revision or of reduced sales.

Project managers and managing editors help to maintain budgets by planning feasible schedules, assessing the work carefully and selecting appropriate people to do it, and checking that everyone for whom they are responsible, including themselves, works to the appropriate standard within the scheduled time.

A word in your ear

There are many styles of communication, from apologetic to apoplectic. To manage projects and teams of people effectively you have to avoid these extremes. While being timid is not an efficient way to get results, being assertive is not a euphemism for rudeness. You can be authoritative without being strident, in control without being intimidating, critical without being unkind. In fact, it is a lot easier for you to get people to do what you want when you want it if you are considerate, calm and supportive. Of course you are under a lot of pressure, and sometimes people or events can really annoy you, but do not make your colleagues the targets for relieving the strain if you want their respect, enthusiasm and cooperation.

5

Effective copy-editing

Copy-editing is a multifaceted job, carrying the tremendous responsibilities of making the author's message clear and accessible to the reader and producing a book at a specified level of quality on schedule and within budget. To do this, you must always keep that message and that reader in mind, be able to select and apply a number and variety of skills appropriately, organize, concentrate and, of course, communicate.

Copy-editors, particularly those who work on illustrated books, are more intimately involved in producing a book than anyone else, and there is a tendency for them to think of each title on which they work as their own. But you must always remember that you are a member of a team, a network of colleagues from whom you receive and to whom you give information so that you can achieve your mutual goal. Like everyone on the team, how well you do your job will influence the ability of the others to do theirs and, ultimately, the quality of the result. However, because you also work directly with more team members than anyone else, your impact on the result, and therefore your responsibility, is greater.

To be able to fulfil your responsibilities and obtain satisfaction from your job you have to be in control of it, not controlled by it. Make the following principles your guidelines.

1 *Take the initiative for all communication*
   - If you need to know, ask: go to the appropriate sources to get information when you need it.
   - If they need to know, tell them: provide information that others need even when they have not asked for it. Warning colleagues of potential changes to schedules or specifications at the earliest opportunity gives the team time to find the best way to cope with a problem rather than leaving it to react to a crisis.
   - If you cannot make contact, leave a message and try again: leaving a message is polite and gives people an opportunity to respond, but when you cannot afford to wait for ever, trying again relieves them of the burden and can produce the result you need.

- If it is important, write it down: written confirmation prevents forgetting or inaccurately remembering aural instructions or agreements; the strongest memory is weaker than the faintest ink. As an editor you should be able to convey information concisely, so writing memos or letters should not take you very long.

2 *Plan your work* Planning what you will do, and how and when you will do it, saves you more time and effort than it takes.

3 *Be flexible* Bear in mind that there may be a number of ways to achieve your ultimate aim so that when circumstances outside your control affect any aspect of your projects — schedules, budgets, specifications — you are prepared to adapt rather than waste time and energy railing against fate.

Look before you leap: assessing manuscripts

However tempting it might be or however much pressure you might be under to start working on a manuscript as soon as it is available, don't. You cannot work effectively if you do not know what you are working on. Assessing the manuscript gives you the information you need to create the detailed schedule and to plan the most efficient approach to the various tasks, and it does not take very long; in fact, the more experienced you become, the less time it takes.

Depending on circumstances, you might be involved in projects during their development or only after the manuscripts are completed, and, sad to say, you might be handed manuscripts without warning and without briefs. If you do not receive full briefs as detailed in Chapter 4 (see page 52–3), ask the commissioning, managing or project editor for essential background information and assess the manuscripts as explained on pages 44–7. Then read on.

Assimilating briefs

Read the entire brief through to familiarize yourself with the project. If it is a good brief, this should not take very long and should give you a general idea of the nature of the book, the reader and the type of work you will be doing. Write down any questions or points of special interest or concern, and note particular reference books or sources you will need to consult.

Now read the brief again. First, imagine yourself as the intended reader: being in that chronological age range, having that reading age and amount of background knowledge, living in the specified markets. Whenever you are working on the project, adopt this mindset to verify what you are doing to the text, illustrations and layout.

Put it in place alongside your professional perspective as you read the specifications and visualize the finished book. Look at any design materials available to help you, such as specimen pages, dummies and flatplans or storyboards. Previously published books in the series, of course, provide a visual template.

Next, examine the project materials as you read the brief. Keep in mind the level of copy-editing — minimal, medial or major (see page 52) — and the other responsibilities as you consider the five main factors below. Make a list of points on which you need more information.

1 *Completeness* Do you have all the elements and are they each complete: the full text, acknowledgements, references, tables, figures, illustration list or roughs, disks, and so on? When are any missing items expected? Can you work around them or will their delay disrupt the schedule? If the schedule is at risk, find out whether the missing elements can be supplied more quickly; otherwise, inform the appropriate people immediately.

2 *Complexity* As you look at the various elements, think about how they interrelate, how you will approach them and at what stage of the process, and how they will affect the speed at which you can work. For example:
   - Are there several styles of list and an apparent need for each of them?
   - Do the tables require arithmetical checking, and are they well laid out or will you have to reorganize them?
   - How extensive is the use of extracts and other quotations and copyright material, and are the acknowledgements in the text or are there references to check?
   - What notation and reference systems have been used and what are the implications for checking cues and citations?
   - Is there documentation to show that permissions have been cleared or sufficient information for you to do this?
   - How extensive is the cross-referencing and is it directional (i.e., above, below, opposite, overleaf) or to numbered figures and tables, page numbers or chapters?
   - Do illustrations need to be keyed in throughout the text?

3 *Presentation* The presentation is no indication of the quality of the content, but you need to consider the following points in terms of their possible impact on the budget and schedule, what you might be able to do to resolve problems and who you need to consult about them.
   - Is the manuscript clean, double-spaced, with adequate margins and dark type, or will you be slowed down by handwritten alterations, typed additions on scraps of paper stapled to the main text, lack of space in which to make your editorial changes, and barely legible type?

- Is the manuscript consecutively numbered? If not, do it after you finish your assessment and before you begin editing.
- Have the disks been checked for compatibility with the systems with which they will be used? If not, have it done immediately and, if they are not compatible, find out the cost and time implications of making them compatible or not using them.
- What does the hard copy reveal about the disk: were formatting guidelines followed or, if not, what are the cost and time implications of stripping out the author's formatting?
- Do you know whether the hard copy and the disk are identical, and if not, which one is the later version?
- Are there separate files on the disk for each chapter, tables, notes, figures and captions?
- Do the notes seem to be prepared in accordance with the agreed system? If not, to what extent will you have revise them?
- Are figures presented as finished artwork or as roughs for which you will have to write briefs and type annotations?
- Is the illustrations list complete and detailed enough to give to a picture researcher or is there more work for you to do?

4 *Text* Read some of the text (see also 'The author's style', below). Does it seem logically organized and at the right level for the reader? Is it verbose or concise, ambiguous or clear, or repetitious? Texts that are dictated tend to suffer from ambiguity and repetition to a greater extent than those that are written by their authors. Do you agree that the briefed level of editing will produce the required quality? If not, work out the implications for the schedule before discussing your view with your manager. If you foresee extensive changes to the text, check whether it will be economical to use the author's disks, and discuss with your manager the implications of changing the production route.

5 *Length* Does the manuscript need cutting or extending and, if so, by how much? If you have not been briefed on this point, do a cast-off now. You can use the computer to provide a word count of each chapter, but if that means checking a large number of files, it could be rather time-consuming. It is quicker to do a rough cast-off on the hard copy.

- Pick a dozen lines of main text at random, and average the number of words in a line.
- Multiply by the number of lines on a page. If the manuscript has been word-processed, there will be a constant number of lines on a full page, otherwise work out the average using several pages at random.

- Multiply that figure by the number of pages in the script. If the pages are not numbered consecutively, add up the extent of the separate chapters. If even those have not been numbered, either count the pages or estimate their number by measuring the height of the manuscript; for example, 500 sheets of average weight (80 gsm) typing paper is about 5 cm (2 inches) high.

The rough cast-off is close enough for you to determine whether you need to trim or add to the manuscript or, if it is excessively (say, 20% or more) over or under the contractual length, that you need to consult your project or commissioning editor. Oh yes, and make a note to provide feedback to the commissioning editor about how helpful it is for authors to number the pages of their manuscript in the manner requested.

Now use the information you have gathered to help you work out how long it will take you to complete each stage.

Scheduling

The following is worth repeating like a mantra. Schedules are one of the driving forces in publishing. Their purpose is to allocate time for people to do their jobs to the required quality in normal working hours, and they play a part in controlling budgets. Take control of your schedules to balance the many facets of your job or they will enslave you.

If you have read the preceding chapters, you will not be surprised that I suggest you make a form with events outside your control highlighted vertically and each project, with its basic specification, listed in the left-hand column. Leave enough space between the entries to allow you to plot the schedule for each function. When the form is filled in with these details, you will be able to see at a glance what you are meant to be doing on all of them at any one time, and what a disruption to any stage of one of them will mean to other stages of that project and to other projects (see Figure 5.1). Thus you will have the ammunition to avoid conflicts and to cope with disruptions when they do occur.

Planning ahead

When you are given advance notice of a project, put the dates of the critical path, the consecutive periods of time that the project is in editorial, design and production, on your schedule, using distinct colours for, or labelling, each function (see pages 47–9. See what effect, if any, these dates have on other work, and consult the editor concerned about any potential problems. Mark a date a couple of weeks

Figure 5.1 A copy-editor's global schedule. Key: *A* = assess; *W* = author; *R* = review

Title and spec	Jan	Feb	Mar	Apr	May	June	July	Aug	Sept	Oct	Nov	Dec
	2 9 16 23 30	6 13 20 27	6 13 20 27	3 10 17 24	1 8 15 22 29	5 12 19 26	3 10 17 24 31	7 14 21 28	4 11 18 25	2 9 16 23 30	6 13 20 27	4 11 18 25
Art History 320 pp. 120.000 words 340 illus	*Edit* / *A*	*W* / *W* / *R*	*Des*	*Set*	*Proofs* / *W* / *Layouts*	*Pages & repro* / *Pic permissions*	*Proofs* / *Index Proof*	*Films O₃*		*Print*	*Public Holiday*	
		Jacket & blad	*Pic research* / *1st selection*									
Portraits 160 pp. 45.000 words 100 illus		*A* / *Edit* / *W* / *Disk* / *W*	*Pic research* / *1st selection W* / *Jacket & blad*	*Des* / *W* / *Index Proof* / *Permissions*	*Page proofs* / *W*	*Repro & films*	*O₃*	*Print*				

Bottom event row (left to right): *New Year · Sales Conference · Bologna Book Fair · Easter · Public Holiday · Publick and Listeners Conference · US Book Fair · Public Holiday · Personnel Time Off · Sales Conference · Book Symposium · Frankfurt Book Fair · Public Holiday · Xmas & New Year*

before you are due to receive the project to remind you to check with the editor that it will arrive on time; your action may remind the editor to check too.

You know that the first thing you are going to do with a project is assess it, so look at the dates immediately after the material is expected, and in a space below the critical path mark off the first week in a colour you will identify with your own work or with an A for 'assessment'. See what your other commitments are during this week, and earmark a specific time in your diary or on your day calendar for this purpose. Keep this appointment as if it were a meeting with the author or another colleague. At first, you might not know how much time to allocate to the appraisal meeting, so start with a couple of hours and monitor yourself over several projects.

Does it fit?

When you have completed the assessment, work out the schedule for each discrete task. Start with the manuscript. Based on the brief and your appraisal, can you estimate how long it will take you to do the first edit and mark-up? The more experience you have and the less varied your work, the easier it is to calculate accurately the amount of time you will need for the different aspects of editing. Whenever your experience is not sufficient, work through a sample of all of the elements about which you feel unsure; perhaps you are not used to revising text to lower the language level, working on a text translated from another language or written by a non-native speaker, or perhaps you have not often worked with references or tables. There are two approaches. For text, it is usually simplest to work on the sample and note how much you have done after, say, four hours of real time — that means including all the usual daily interruptions for telephone conversations, informal discussions with colleagues, coffee or tea breaks and so on. For a collection of separate items, like tables, it is easier to measure how long it takes in real time to work through a few representative ones. Either way, you can then calculate the approximate amount of time for the whole based on the time needed for the sample. But it was only a sample, so add some contingency time.

Contingency time is just what the name indicates: time needed to cope with the unexpected, with problems that cannot be foreseen, as opposed to the ones that could have been foreseen if only someone had been looking forward and thinking. You probably do not need to add more than a day or two at any stage. Adhere to the principle of assessing a realistic amount of time to do each job and you won't fall into the trap of using this time for anything other than emergencies.

Let us say that you estimate it will take three weeks to do the first edit of script A *if you work on nothing else*. 'Aha!' you say. 'But I do work on something else.' Yes, most people do, and we will work that into the calculation, but first we need to collect a few more numbers. Therefore, ask yourself how long it will take for the author to respond to the queries you raise. Don't simply guess. Estimate the time by considering the number and nature of the queries likely to arise from this script combined with what you know about the author. For example:

- Are the questions going to be few or many, simple or complex?
- Will the author be able to answer them from what he or she is expected to know or will research be necessary, and are the answers likely to be long or short?
- Is the author's time for dealing with your queries restricted by his or her job?
- Does the author have a reputation for attending to such matters quickly or slowly?

Be sure to allow time for the questions to reach the author and for the answers to reach you if they are sent in the mail; obviously the time taken by fax or e-mail is insignificant, but not everyone has these facilities. Add *a little* contingency time. Let us say that you estimate the question-and-answer stage will take two weeks.

How much time will you need for the second edit? Take into account:

- how many answers there are to incorporate,
- whether they are likely to be typed or handwritten,
- whether they are likely to be sufficient in themselves or require further editing or research by you,
- how much writing or keyboarding you will need to do,
- whether you will need to produce a new printout,
- how long it will take to read through the script again.

Say a week for the second edit.

Perhaps your manager has told you to set aside a few days for him or her to check the edited manuscript before it goes to design: add a week, to allow for the reading and for you to make any final revisions. Are you also obliged to send the author the script at this stage? If you maintain good communication with the author during the editing, you can send it as confirmation of what you have already agreed rather than providing an opportunity for rewriting. Then the author can read a copy of the script at the same time as the manager and not affect the schedule.

Now that you have the numbers, you can fill in the schedule. Look at the dates for the editing stage on the critical path. Let's say there are 14 weeks between your receipt of the project and the date when it must go to design (see also 'When it's too tight', below). What is the last task before that? Working in the space below the critical path, the one in which you marked a week for assessment, draw a band through the week that you have allocated for the manager to read and you to revise the script; maybe you want to mark it R for 'read and revise' or use a particular colour for this function.

You have 12 weeks left, of which you need six: three for the first edit, two for querying and one for the second edit. You are given more time than the job itself takes because you are working on more than one job. You need to spread the time it takes to do any one task over a greater period of time according to what your other simultaneous commitments are. For example, you could count off seven weeks after the assessment on the critical path line for the first edit. In the space below, and in a colour or a label designated for the author, you would then mark the two weeks for the querying stage: you have already taken the author's other commitments into account in estimating the time needed here, so do not increase it. That would leave three weeks for the second edit before the manager sees the manuscript.

A time for every purpose

Move down the line to the next editorial stage: proofs. Allocate time on the critical path line for you to read the first proofs — or on a line below if they will be read by another person — and to collate the proofs. Mark the author's dates for receiving and returning proofs on a separate line. This reminds you to give the author advance notice of when the proofs will be coming and when they need to be returned; remember to check the contract for how long the author is allowed and to make sure the return date gives you sufficient time for collating. Allocate time for all proof stages in this way, noting when the author gets proofs to read and return and when for information only.

Analyse all the elements for which you are responsible in the same way. Give a separate line to each one because they are not sequential but overlapping. For example, on a separate line mark in and label the dates for picture research:

- brief picture researcher (see also Chapter 7),
- first selection meeting with picture researcher, author, designer,
- final selection,
- keyed into script/proof; handover to design/production,
- proofs in (if you do not know, ask design or production whether photos will be scatterproofed or seen only imposed on page),
- corrected proofs out.

If you are doing the picture research yourself, you will need to allocate time for preparing the picture credits and sending back pictures after publication.

On another line schedule the artwork:

- prepare briefs,
- handover meeting with designer/illustrator,
- artist's roughs due; contact author,
- author's comments due,
- corrections to illustrator,
- final artwork in,

- keyed into script/proof; handover to design/production,
- proofs in (if you do not know, ask design or production whether colour artwork will be scatterproofed or seen only imposed on page),
- corrected proofs out.

Follow the same principles for analysing and assigning time to briefing, checking and proofreading the index; briefing the designer for commissioned photography, working on the jacket and blad (see 'Co-editions', below, and Chapter 11), and checking their proof stages. Compare the dates for all the elements to make sure they coordinate with each other where necessary and with those on the critical path.

Now change your focus; look at the global schedule. Have you accounted for the effect of all the highlighted dates? If not, make the necessary adjustments, always checking the impact on the entire schedule both vertically and horizontally. Look again. Are there periods when it looks as though you will be doing too many jobs simultaneously? If so, move some tasks to a different range of dates until they all work, or ask for assistance.

Even when you have worked out the schedules to allow sufficient time for every task, you may find them difficult to maintain because some authors or colleagues are prone to delays. Checking in advance that material will be handed over on time can help to reduce the size of the problem. Notice, too, whether individuals have a pattern of delay; for example, is it always a certain number of days or does it occur only when the handover is scheduled for a Friday? The common way to overcome the first problem is to make contingency time for those colleagues … without telling them. Give them dates that are realistic, but plan your schedule in the knowledge that the work will arrive later. You can also try to help them break the habit. Explain that you have noticed that they are often a bit late, so this time you have put an extra day in the schedule. Keep your contingency time, of course, but see if your tardy colleagues are able to respond by being that one day closer to the schedule. Give them time to get used to that, then try again.

Friday schedules are psychologically a poor bet. Usually, nothing happens to the work over the weekend, so some people get in the habit of reading Monday afternoon for Friday morning. Try to schedule handover dates for Thursday if you really want to work on the material on Friday, or for Monday morning if that is the earliest it will be used.

When it's too tight

There may be occasions when your project assessment and schedule analysis reveal that you do not have enough time to produce the work to the accepted standard within normal working hours. This can be because the critical path time is actually too short or, since most editors work on a number of projects simultaneously, because of the pressure of other tasks.

Never pretend — to yourself or anyone else — that you can do something when you know you cannot. Instead, think about the most appropriate action to take. If the critical path time is insufficient — that 400-page badly written text cannot be edited in five normal working days — determine how much more is needed, keeping contingency time to the bare minimum. Consult your colleagues in design and production: do they have enough time to do their tasks, and if so, can they reduce it so that you can have more? If that does not prove successful, discuss the situation with your manager, explaining your analysis and your attempted solution. Maybe the schedule will be renegotiated or, if it cannot be — perhaps publication is tied to a TV series, film release or special event — you will be told to work faster to a lower standard, or the manager will pass the project to someone else.

When the pressure of other tasks reduces the time available, see whether you can make the time you need by adjusting those schedules, consulting your design and production colleagues when necessary. When shuffling the schedules does not work, talk to your manager about getting someone else to do certain tasks to release your time. The manager will have to see whether someone in-house can help or whether the budget will permit a freelancer to be employed.

It is also possible that, in response to a request for assistance or more time, you will be told that 'normal' working hours are as many as it takes to do the job and that you can complete the particular task by working longer than regular office hours. Can you? Sure, lots of people put in extra time occasionally, but you must make a considered judgement before you agree to do so. First, how much extra time is required and, second, how much energy do you have? A few hours one night or spread through the week probably will not exhaust you, but working until midnight daily and over the weekend might. As you get more tired, you will work more slowly and the quality of your work will diminish. And if you work seven days without a break, how will it affect your work the following week? Measure the time required against your energy levels (be honest and realistic) to decide whether the effort will be counterproductive.

Overtime: occasionally or habitually?

When you decide that you can work overtime, you need to consider whether you want to or should. Most team workers are willing to put in an extra effort from time to time; they may get paid for it or be given time off in compensation, or accept satisfaction at overcoming a hurdle as their reward. However, if the need to work overtime is not occasional but constant, something is wrong. It is fair to ask whether you are working too slowly because you are underskilled, in which case you should be given the requisite training, or whether you have been given too much work because the company is understaffed, in which case you are being exploited. Compare yourself to other people doing a similar job:

1 Are you the only one regularly working late?
2 Do you have the same sized workload as your colleagues?
3 Do you suspect or know that you are not adequately trained in some skills?

If the answer to 1 and 2 is yes, so is the answer to 3 in all probability. In this case, ask for the help you need. Your manager may be able to train you her- or himself, arrange for you to go on an external course, or realize that there are others who would benefit from the same training and arrange for a course to be provided in-house. A company that does not offer any kind of training is not investing in its employees or, by extension, in itself. Think about your future.

If you are freelance, you are your own manager and therefore the primary responsibility for training is yours. Just as you expect the plumber you hire to know how to install a sink, a publishing company employs freelancers for the skills they have, not the training they need. Think about your future too.

If you are working late because you have a heavier workload than anyone else, talk to your manager to see if some work can be redistributed. On the other hand, if everyone is working late, the discussion should focus on the possibility of extending schedules to lighten the load or the company's policy on staffing and using freelance help.

Principles of copy-editing

You have assimilated the brief, assessed the work and planned the schedule: you know what you have to do and how long you have to do it. How you do it will determine whether you achieve the quality required and maintain the budget, the schedule and good working relationships with your colleagues.

Rules and alternatives

A brief tells you the particular requirements of a project, not the full extent or limit of your responsibilities. You are expected to know what they are; if you are in any doubt, ask, don't guess or assume. You are also expected to have, and know how to apply, various skills to meet those responsibilities. Of course, no one knows everything or remembers all they know all the time, which is why effective professionals have and use the appropriate reference materials.

Copy-editing handbooks, manuals of style, grammar books and dictionaries supply much of the basic information you need to do your job. They can tell you something you did not know or confirm something you thought you did. Never be afraid to use them, but be aware that in many instances they are a guide rather than the gospel. A comparison of several books in many of these categories will show you that there are some points on which they all agree — the rules — and many on which they do not — the alternatives. The fact that alternatives exist means you have to make choices. A comprehensive house style makes many of these choices for you, but, unfortunately, not all publishers have a house style, let alone a comprehensive one. And even when you have a set of rules, you have to know when and how far to bend them.

The choice of alternatives or how you bend the rules will depend on your evaluation of the effect on the author's message and its impact on the reader, and efficiency. For example, the text might deviate from the accepted practice on spelling or capitalizing certain words. Before you change it, find out whether the variations are essential to the purpose of the book or unintentional errors (see 'Surely not', below). Maybe the references do not list all the bibliographic information in the usual order. Before you change them, look at them with the reader's mindset: does the order present any impediment to understanding? If not, you might still decide to alter them, to maintain house style, if there are only a few, but to leave them alone if there are a great many and they are consistent.

The author's style

Everyone has an individual voice, a way of using words. We can recognize people not only by the sound of their voice but also by their pattern of speech. The words they choose might convey only information and ideas, but their tone of voice reveals their emotional attitude. These oral characteristics have a written equivalent: the author's style.

Books with a multiplicity of contributors, such as encyclopedias, dictionaries and various other reference books, and many textbooks have a consistent tone and an anonymous voice; one purpose of the editing is to remove individuality. The information is primary and the authority rests mainly or entirely in the reputation of the publisher. In other books, however, unless you have been briefed to suppress the author's style, your responsibility is to maintain it or modify it only to the extent necessary to make it suitable for the intended audience. You must still, of course, correct grammar and usage, improve organization at all levels, remove unnecessary repetition and irrelevancies, clarify ambiguity, and ensure accuracy and consistency. You must also alter statements that would break the law, lead to unsafe practice, or be parochial or otherwise inappropriate for the intended market. What you must not do is change the author's text because you do not like it.

The good copy-editor has been everywhere and is revealed nowhere in the finished book. Your job is to help authors to transmit *their* message, and it is not their message if you put it in your voice. It is possible, and often necessary, to improve an author's style, but you can do this only if you recognize it and know the difference between enhancing it and supplanting it.

When you read for pleasure you absorb the author's style as you progress through the book. When you are editing, you must understand the author's style before you can proceed, and it is often expedient, particularly with the work of inexperienced authors, to focus on the middle of the manuscript for this purpose.

Start by *listening* to the text. Hear its rhythm: is it rolling, flowing, rambling, staccato or mixed? Feel its tempo: racing, quick, leisurely or slow? Some people's voices are stronger than others, so you may have to listen carefully to pick up a whispered style. Wait until you have grasped these effects, then look at the structure to see how it creates them. Are the paragraphs long or short? Are the sentences simple, compound or complex, syntactically varied or uniform, passive or active? Does the punctuation control or confuse, enhance or inhibit?

Listen to the author's tone: is it impersonal, enthusiastic, manic, patronizing, uncertain, natural, stilted? Look at the proportions of the different kinds of word and device used that contribute to it: adverbs and adjectives; comparatives and superlatives; present participles; multisyllabic, obscure, vogue or foreign words, metaphors and similes. Look at the words themselves. Familiarize yourself with the vocabulary the author uses, including pet words or phrases, idioms, and unusual expressions.

In nonfiction the copy-editor helps make the author's style consistent throughout the text, although the tone may vary. In fiction, however, authors may use their own voice for narration, and create distinct voices for their characters. Skilful writers make speech reflect each character's individuality — age, level of education, social group, occupation, origins and personality — just as it does in reality. It is essential that the copy-editor hears and maintains the voice of each character as well as that of the author.

When you have identified the style, think about its overall effect. The way an author writes can make a 'dry' subject interesting, an interesting one boring; it can invite readers in, push them away or be indifferent. Look at which elements promote and which impair the clarity of the author's message or the purpose of the book. As you edit, you can modify the style as well as the content as long as you *always, always, always* do it to make the author's message clear to the reader, and let the author know what you are doing. Thus when you decide to change one word or phrase for another, alter the syntax, or reorganize the paragraph or chapter, it will be for sound reasons, such as accuracy, precision, clarity, avoidance of repetition, and consistency of characterization. The change must be an improvement, not merely your preference.

Author and baby care 1: who are they?

Copy-editing is a pleasure when you have the author on your side. It's where he or she belongs, too, because you have the same objective: producing a book that will sell. But never forget that it is not just any book, but the author's book. An author may be contracted because she or he is an authority on a subject although not a writer, or a journalist who can write at a superficial level on a variety of subjects; or because he or she tells stories of a certain genre or has produced a novel that the commissioning editor believes will sell for any of a dozen reasons. Whatever category the author is in, respect him or her for producing the manuscript; believe me, even if the result is not great, it was not easy.

Writing is a creative process and while not all authors regard themselves as artists, most of them feel like parents sending their child away to … to what? If noone has explained the process to them, novices may expect the company simply to print their book (put their baby on the stage); others may realize that at least the spelling and grammar will be corrected first (baby will be cleaned and tidied up); while those who have published before may be familiar with copy-editing and have a negative (baby will be battered or a changeling) or positive (that's my baby, what a star!) view of it, depending on their experiences. Parents naturally feel protective; they should not be made to feel defensive.

Author and baby care 2: who are you?

Until you introduce yourself, you are a stranger. Maybe, and only maybe, someone has told the authors that you will be copy-editing their script. That prepares the way, but you are still just a name. Begin to establish a relationship with your authors by letting them know who you are and what is going to happen and when. Do not be intimidated by an author's status or reputation, and do not patronize those new to the publishing world. Treat all of them as you wish to be treated: as a professional.

Unless you have been told to phone, it is usually better to write to authors initially. You can invite them to phone you if they like or let them know that you will be phoning them for a particular purpose, for example to discuss points in the script or to arrange a meeting. It is sensible to ask them for the most convenient time to reach them, as the majority of authors have other jobs and are not necessarily always available, and those who write for a living might not want to be interrupted.

Start by putting yourself in context, linking yourself to someone the authors know, their commissioning editor, for example, or the company if you are a freelancer: 'X has asked me to copy-edit your manuscript.' Add remarks about how pleased you are to do this or what a wonderful manuscript it is only if you are sincere; sycophancy and hypocrisy have a distinct odour.

What you know about the authors' background influences how you tell them what is going to happen. For example, 'As you know,' or 'As you may know,' or, without preamble, 'The first thing we have to do is meet to discuss the illustrations' or 'As well as making sure the text is consistent with house style, copy-editing usually raises some queries that only the author can answer.'

Your earliest opportunity to convey this information is after you have finished the assessment. Large projects on a long schedule mean that you can give authors advance notice, so they can arrange to attend the meeting or prepare themselves to respond to queries without delay. 'We would like to have the meeting at x or y time. Please let me know which is more convenient for you or if another time would be more suitable'; 'I will send the queries for several chapters at a time at intervals of about three weeks, starting three weeks from now. Please let me know if there is any time between x and y when you will be unable to respond.' Authors who tell you which dates will be affected give you the chance to plan for a possible delay that otherwise could be a disruption.

Shorter schedules do not allow either party much room for manoeuvre, so you need to keep control gracefully: 'As you know, we want to publish your book in …, so we need to have the meeting on x or y. Please let me know which is more convenient for you'; 'I will send you the queries for the first half of the book next week, and the remaining ones the week after. It would be a big help if you could return them at weekly intervals too, but if not, we can still keep the schedule if you return them by x. Please let me know as soon as possible if this presents a problem.'

You have opened the channels of communication and shown that you are in control and considerate. The authors can relax a little: they are in safe hands. Now, what about baby?

Surely not

Always remember that the authors' names, not yours, appear on the title page and cover. Whether you agree with what they say or like the way they say it is irrelevant. As long as the text does not contravene any laws or company policy, your job is to make *the authors'* message accessible to the readers. (Yes, that has been said elsewhere and is worth repeating.) Authors are usually pleased at improvements to the text, especially when errors are corrected before publication, because they know that the quality of the text can affect their reputation and the potential sales of the book. Obviously, you must have their agreement to changes in the manuscripts, and how you handle this procedure can enhance or impair your relationship. By informing authors of what you are proposing to do rather than showing them what you have done, you avoid the risks of antagonizing them and of wasting time making changes that have to be unmade at a later, and by definition, more expensive stage.

If authors have never seen the house style, in your introductory letter explain what kind of alterations to their manuscript it implies. Authors might respond by ignoring references to points about which they are not concerned, say the style of quotation marks or abbreviations or the representation of numbers, but expressing their strong views on retaining certain variant spellings, capitalizations, or scientific or technical nomenclature.

Clearly, only the authors can resolve ambiguities and tell you the sources of quoted material, and although you can make suggestions, only they can make decisions that affect the product of their imagination — characters, plots, locations. However, you have to ensure the accuracy of information that is based in reality, even when it is in a fictional context. Naturally, you will check various sources and then write to the author. Do not impede your own work by being vague, even if you are in a hurry. Avoid asking a general question, like 'Is this paragraph all right?' Authors might say yes because they do not know what your concern is, and later object to that very issue, or they might rewrite another part of the paragraph unnecessarily. Even when you narrow the question to a specific point, word each query precisely, and concisely, to focus the authors' attention and minimize the chances of getting an answer to a question you did not ask.

A tried and tested way of sabotaging your relationship with authors is to write 'Surely, you mean …'. Enough editors have made this mistake to satisfy cruel fate; you can be spared. First, think about the quality and currency of the sources you are using, especially when they contradict the authors' text. Dictionaries, atlases and encyclopedias are years in the making, and some of the information they contain can be out of date by the time they are published. Articles and books by other authors might also be out of date, particularly in fields where change is a constant factor, and contain different opinions about so-called facts. Errors can creep into any publication. Perhaps the reason your authors' text is different from published sources is because they have a different interpretation of the issue or are the first to publish new findings. 'Surely' is not the case.

Next, think about what you are querying or commenting on, an issue in the text, not the authors. 'Surely, you mean' attacks the authors; they are bound to be defensive rather than cooperative. There is, of course, no need to attack at all. Your role is to call attention to issues, to solicit answers or agreement to changes. Smooth your path with objectivity. Point out that the text, not the author, says *x* but other sources say *y*, and inquire whether it should be altered or not. The objective tone of the question allows authors to consider it without embarrassment. You are both examining and trying to improve an inanimate object. Authors might respond by explaining why their text differs from others, by clarifying the statement or simply by agreeing to the amendment.

You can make it easy for authors to accept necessary change in their work by writing in their style. For example, when you explain that a piece of text needs to be clarified, expanded or condensed, you can *offer* the wording. If authors hear their own voice, and the revised text is correct, although they are under no obligation, they are more likely to accept it than try to replace it. This means fewer author rewrites to edit, which helps to maintain textual consistency as well as the schedule and the budget.

You will, of course, be careful not to alter the authors' meaning by the changes you suggest to words or organization. You will test the necessity and desirability of repetition with the readers' mindset before you suggest deletions, and you will tactfully inquire whether and how that which appears irrelevant can be made pertinent. You know your job.

Unplanned changes

Your well-laid plans can be upset by changes to the project that are unexpected in time or scale. Authors, for example, might prevail on their commissioning editors to be allowed to make extensive changes or even rewrite at galley or page proof, or to include more text or illustrations than previously specified. Commissioning editors might be inclined to agree because part of their job is to support their authors. Part of your job is to advise commissioning editors to what extent the changes requested will make a difference to the sales of the book, and to the budget and the schedule. Take a balanced view. Supporting authors *is* important and sometimes late changes are beneficial, but delaying publication harms sales and exceeding the budget reduces profits. See if there are ways to minimize the impact on schedules and budgets, and be sure to draw designers and production controllers into the discussion. Well-reasoned responses to requests for changes make it easier for commissioning editors and authors to make informed decisions about which alterations are really important.

Co-editions

Highly illustrated books are expensive to produce and are viable only when the print runs are high and the costs are shared among a number of publishers in different countries. To succeed before and after publication, these co-editions must not betray their country of origin in words or illustrations. Although the co-publishers have to translate the text, they do not expect to research and rewrite it to replace irrelevant or inappropriate references, and they do not budget for it. It is your responsibility to be aware of and to delete or replace text that does not travel: idioms, colloquialisms, references to local habits and customs, brand names, types of organization, educational and legal systems, and general ethnocentricity. Similarly, because co-editions are predicated on the common use of the illustrations, you need to look for and exclude images that are unnecessarily parochial and ensure that there is no design feature that would preclude producing different editions by changing only the black text plate.

Avoidance is not always enough to make a book acceptable to readers in each market. In subjects where the evidence is not limited to one country there must be content with which readers everywhere can identify. However, including lists of examples and images from all the intended markets every time a textual or visual illustration is needed makes a book tedious and bland. Balance is the goal. You help authors attain it by editing the text, selecting photographs and briefing artwork so that examples are suitably varied.

To develop the mindset of the universal reader, essential for working on co-editions, you have to learn about the dislikes and taboos of different cultures: what is not eaten, what is not done, what may not be depicted. Analyse existing books to see why they did or could not succeed as co-editions. Ask for guidelines or specific advice from colleagues with relevant experience — not only editors, but also designers, picture researchers and rights personnel. Generally, the co-publishers expect to have minimal involvement, and depend on you to produce the right material. However, if other avenues have failed to remove doubts about an issue in text or illustrations, liaise with your opposite number rather than make assumptions or take chances that could require costly and time-consuming changes later. Co-edition partners will be more favourably impressed by this perceptive consideration of their publishing needs than by your ability to amend oversights.

Co-editions complicate schedules. Co-publishers need the edited text, including captions and annotations on artwork, to translate, edit and proof, and they need to see illustrations and finished layouts or pages for the same reasons you do. They may need to see the jacket design for approval or be supplied with images to use in creating their own design. And they need all this in sufficient time to prepare their film to print their edition with yours. In addition, you will probably have to produce a blad (see Chapter 11). You know how to stay in control: put the dates for supplying materials to other publishers on your global schedule and make the usual adjustments if they are affected by external events or impact on the schedules for other projects. Confirm dates for the flow of materials with your colleagues in the other firms, inform them as far in advance as possible of any changes, and ask them to let you know if they need to alter any dates.

Briefing indexers

Although indexers are almost always freelance, how to brief them is included here because it is usually your job. See Chapter 9 for the general principles of working with freelancers.

All nonfiction books should have an index to enable readers to find information quickly and easily. Indexes are tools of accessibility. If they are poorly made and cannot do the job for which they are intended, they frustrate the readers. Simply put, a bad index diminishes a book. Even those publishing houses that require authors to provide their own indexes recognize that the majority of them lack the objectivity, the training and the time essential for this vital task. They accept that authors may pay for, but professionals will prepare the indexes. In houses that pay for the indexes, commissioning editors budget for them in the proposals. You, as always, are responsible for maintaining the budget and schedule, and ensuring the quality. How good the indexes are will depend on the skill of the indexers you choose and the briefs you give them.

To facilitate the indexers' work and minimize your own, the brief should be written and should state:

- subject and intended audience,
- types of index,
- levels of subentry,
- use of cross-references,
- layout and length,
- house style for capitalization, page references to text and to illustrations, elision of numerals, and punctuation,
- presentation of completed index,
- schedule,
- terms and conditions.

How many and what kinds of index a book should have and how complex they should be will depend on the subject and approach, the needs of the intended audience, and what the budget and space allow. The number and type might be stated in the original proposal or the brief you received from the commissioning editor. Otherwise your first job is to decide what needs to be indexed. The categories, from the most common to the most specialized, include:

- subject
- personal and other proper names
- first lines of poems
- titles, for example of books, poems, or works of art

- authors
- recipes
- ingredients
- methods or techniques
- common plant names
- botanical names
- place names
- legal cases
- legislation

Several categories can be combined or all can be kept separate. Discuss the categories and content with the authors, who may have a clear vision of what is needed even though they are not providing it themselves.

All entries should be substantive, not peripheral. The purpose is to lead the readers to information rather than the occurrence of words. Decide whether the treatment of the text and the needs of the readers require main entries only or one or two levels of subentry, which will influence the use of cross-references. If there is only one level of subentry, you can choose between a run on or broken off layout, but if there are two levels of subentry, each subentry must be broken off (start on a new indented line), while the sub-subentries can be run on or broken off. In addition, the indexer needs to know how much to indent subentries and turnover lines.

The amount of space available will also influence the final decision on subentry levels and layout. Proposals specify an extent, and the number and ratio of words and illustrations. Based on these numbers and the typographic specification, designers can work out at an early stage how many pages the text and illustrations will occupy and how many are allowed for the index. Brief them to design the index, so that you can tell the indexer the number of:

- characters to a line,
- lines to a column,
- columns to a page, and
- pages.

By typing to the line measure and counting the number of lines, the indexer can produce an index that fits the space, avoiding the need for cuts to be made by you. Knowing the subject and the reader as you do, you might be able to estimate whether the space is sufficient for the style of index you are planning before you brief the indexer, or you might have to ask the indexer to assess this for you. If there is a mismatch between style and space, decide how you can alter the former, or discuss with the designer how to create more of the latter (see Chapter 6).

Do you have a house style for indexes? If so, read it through and make sure it contains all the information the indexer needs for the present index. Remove irrelevant points, add missing details and emphasize any that are unusual and to which you wish to call special attention.

Like manuscripts, indexes should be presented as double-spaced hard copy. If the indexers are also supplying disks, brief them on formatting and coding indentations, bold and italics for compatibility with the house system, and to ensure that the hard copy is the same version as on the disks. Do not assume that you can skip the editing stage: computers do not necessarily mean perfection. Make sure that you have allowed yourself sufficient time in the schedule to edit the index.

Check that the indexer has read and understood the brief, agrees that the schedule is adequate, and that the terms and conditions are acceptable. If the brief is good and the indexer follows it, the editing will be easy.

6

Working with designers

The omnipresence of the computer and the plethora of graphic design software have led many people to mistake the tool for the skill. It is astounding that publishing companies that would not consider hiring as a designer a person without relevant qualifications in design would allow, let alone require, editors without adequate knowledge of book design to take on any part of this role. The ability to manipulate a program on computer does not automatically bestow competence in the principles of design. If you cannot design without the computer, you cannot design with it. To the untutored, the multitude of typefaces, the ease of using italics and bold, or centring, justifying, ranging and shaping text are playthings, whereas in the hands of a professional they are instruments of efficiency. Rather than trying to do their job, you need to understand what designers do and what their perspective is so that you can work together effectively.

Now you see it

Designers give books their visual appearance. Good design, like good copy-editing, is invisible. It does not scream 'Look at me', but makes the authors' message visually accessible to the reader. It might bellow that message or state it calmly, grab the readers or entice them, be exciting or conservative, avant-garde or traditional. What makes it good — *skilful*, not necessarily pretty or elegant — is that it serves its purpose: it appeals to and works for the intended reader. Whether it is to your personal taste is, of course, irrelevant.

All books need to be designed, but how early in the production process that happens depends on the kind of publishing and, as always, to some extent on the company and the individuals in it. In format publishing, designers are involved in the beginning to establish a limited number of detailed page designs that will satisfy the needs of all the company's books. After that, all the editors know which books come into which category and follow the set pattern in commissioning and copy-editing. Copy-editors may commission diagrams and size illustrations, while page layout is commonly done by the printer. Contact with designers is minimal, as they are usually employed only to produce covers and jackets.

In text-only and unintegrated illustrated publishing it is common for designers to determine the look of the page when they have the edited manuscripts. As commissioning editor, you should consult them, when necessary, to make sure that the number of words you want to commission will fit into the extent you are planning in a typesize suitable to the audience, but which font, what size, how much leading, and other details of the page can wait until later.

Integrated illustrated books that are individual in style are more dependent on visual appearance for their success than the types of book mentioned above. The earlier designers are involved, the more helpful they can be and the better the result is likely to be. At the very beginning, when the project is still an idea aimed at a particular market, discussing with designers what you are trying to accomplish can help you to work out the specifications faster and often more satisfactorily than if you tried to make all the choices alone. Designers can also define the details of the typography and the general page layout at this stage, which can facilitate commissioning, writing and copy-editing. Books produced in this way are often referred to as design-led, which, when the result is the combined effort of designers and editors, does not mean design-dominated. Alternatively, this collaboration can take place when the manuscript is in-house, before, during or after editing, depending on the schedule. To be successful, this process, whenever it occurs, requires at least two participants to exchange information and ideas. Be prepared to give facts and reasoned opinion, ask for the same, listen to what is said with an open mind, and then repeat the process until you are satisfied with the result.

What they do and what they don't

Just as you need to understand the extent and limits of your own job, you should understand what designers are and are not expected to do. The list of negatives is shorter, so let's start with it. Designers do not necessarily do any of the following.

1 *Read the text* This does not mean they cannot, it means they are not paid to spend their time doing so. This principle underlies all the other negatives and explains why editors have to mark-up text and provide briefs.

2 *Know what illustrations are needed or provide references for them* They cannot commission illustrators or photographers until you provide briefs. If reference material is needed, you must produce it (see 'Artwork' and 'Photography', below).

3 *Know where illustrations belong* You must key all illustrative materials into the manuscript or proofs.

4 *Check content of artwork and commissioned photographs* Examining work for conformity to the brief is your job (see ' Artwork' and 'Photography', below).

5 *Write captions* How could they? They don't know what is in the text and may not understand the content or know the point of the illustrations.

6 *Cut or fill text* They could just drop overmatter or repeat the last lines until the column or page is filled, but that is hardly the effect we want.

Free of these irrelevancies, designers can do the following jobs.

1 *Create the grid* Commissioning editors usually stipulate the page size, but designers determine the text area and how it is organized. The purpose of the grid is to ensure visual consistency, so it shows the elements that are common to all pages:

- the trimmed page and, where relevant, the bleed,
- the number and width of columns,
- the depth of, and number of lines in, a column,
- the relative sizes of the margins,
- the positioning of folios and running heads.

Grids are usually produced for spreads to show the relationship of the features on the recto and verso. In simple designs, one page of the grid can be used to detail the positioning of the chapter heading, epigraph and first line of text. In books of greater complexity, separate grids may be needed for the distinct sections. In some design-led books, particularly spread-by-spread titles and those with many contributors providing fairly short articles, grids can be given to authors to help them write the correct amount and remind them to provide the necessary number of illustrations.

You should look at grids to see that there is sufficient margin space for the reader to hold the book without obscuring the text and that folios and running heads are positioned for easy reference.

2 *Plan typography* The typeface and size and the amount of leading determine how dense the text will look and must be appropriate to the subject and suitable for the reader. Designers have to use the typography to indicate the structure of the elements on the page. It takes great skill to design complex pages with, say, main text and three levels of heading, prose extracts, verse, tables, annotated figures, footnotes and captions and make them harmonious. Sample, or specimen, pages of typographic design can help authors to stick to a structural pattern as they write, and can aid those copy-editors who find it difficult to make final decisions because they cannot visualize the typeset page. Look at these pages with the reader's mindset: is everything clear, legible, accessible?

3 *Cast off text* When grids are constructed before the text is written, your cast-off to determine whether the manuscript complies with the terms of the contract or

whether it needs cutting or expanding is sufficient. When the grid is drawn after the receipt of manuscript, the designer's cast-off is more accurate for copyfitting purposes because it is based on characters rather than words.

4 *Flat-plan* The simplest flat-plan indicates where colour is available in a book that is not totally monochrome or four-colour. Designers can create more detailed flat-plans to show the flow of text and pictures throughout the volume. In many cases they can do so before the manuscript is edited, and even before it is written.

5 *Commission and supervise photography* Designers can hire photographers, locations and necessary additional personnel, such as stylists, models and home economists, and organize them to do their jobs on time and within budget. To get appropriate people and produce the results you want, designers need good editorial briefs (see 'Photography', below). You check the content of the photos, designers check the quality.

6 *Commission illustrators* Some editors, especially those in children's books, do this job themselves. Elsewhere, designers hire illustrators to produce artwork in the style that you have agreed with them is suitable for the book and the reader. You provide the brief and references for the content (see 'Artwork', below), while designers provide the brief for materials and technical preparation. You each check what you briefed. They are responsible for negotiating the fees and maintaining the schedule.

7 *Lay out pages* Designers can use paper, scissors and paste or sophisticated computer software to position all textual and illustrative matter on the pages, as long as you indicate which pictures belong near which words. The grids are their templates and they have a responsibility for maintaining visual consistency in producing layouts or page proofs, which you will also check. When designers are not producing the pages on computer themselves, they will check the printer's proofs for consistency. They will also check high-resolution proofs of the illustrations to see that the images have been correctly sized and cropped, and that the quality of reproduction is satisfactory.

8 *Design jackets and covers* These essential sales tools often have to be designed before the book is typeset and laid out. You have to provide the general brief, maybe illustrations, and certainly all the words to be incorporated.

Designers, like editors, can have different job titles, depending on where they work and what they do: design director, art director, design manager, senior designer, layout artist; for simplicity, the text refers to them collectively as designers. Several designers might work on a single project: one might create the grid and typography, another be responsible for commissioning illustrations and preparing page layouts, and a third specialize in jackets and covers. Remember to brief each of them appropriately.

Briefing books

It should be evident by now that designers cannot do their job in a vacuum. Like you, they need to know what materials they have to work with and who the audience is. They may be given parts of this information at different times — some when they are helping to determine the specifications, more when they are preparing specimen pages, and final details when they are processing the materials — or all at once if they are involved only in the last-mentioned stage. Figure 6.1 presents the elements in a complete design brief as a checklist, although, as the text below reveals, a checklist is only a starting point; to get the best results, there must be discussion. Always try to keep information as concise and as clear as possible. Keep a copy of all written briefs so that you can confer with distant colleagues easily, be sure that everyone agrees on what was commissioned, and replace lost briefs without delay or difficulty.

Subject and reader

To start to visualize a project, designers need to know the subject and whether it is a single title or the beginning of a series. For example, they may begin to see a landscape format for a single children's book about building a submarine, but think differently if they know that another title in the series will be about building a skyscraper; they might envision one typeface for a single volume on pop art, but another if the series is going to include books on Renaissance, Gothic and Impressionist art.

The category of reader greatly influences typography and the level of design. Even if the subject is the same, the typeface, size, leading and measure and the sophistication of illustrations would be different for children in different age groups and with different reading abilities, different for adults generally, and for professionals and academics.

Books for domestic consumption may be designed and illustrated in styles that appeal to national tastes, while co-editions must avoid all visual parochialism. Designers experienced in co-edition publishing (always choose people with appropriate skills and experience unless you have sufficient time and experience to train them) know that, to succeed, the grid and typography have to accommodate languages that make the original text longer or shorter, that the use of colour and reversing out are restricted in specific ways, and that annotated artwork should be prepared on a separate overlay. They may expect to be asked to create a colour flatplan before the proposal is accepted and, realizing the implications for producing blads and providing publishing partners with final layouts, want to discuss the schedule with you. Make sure this discussion takes place: initiate it.

1 Series: _____

2 Subject/title: _____

3 Market
   • age range: _____
   • reading level: _____
   • domestic/coedition: _____

4 Specifications
   • format: _____ × _____ mm/inches
   • extent: _____ pp
   • number of words: _____
   • number of illustrations: _____
   • inserts/integrated
   • use of colour: ___ × ___
   • hardback/softback/looseleaf/spiral
   • cover/jacket

5 Structure and detail
   • spread-by-spread/continuous
   • heading levels: part ___, chapter ____, A– ___
   • types of text included: _____
   • special features in text: _____
   • special features in prelims/endmatter: _____

6 No. of photographs
   • commissioned _____
   • sourced _____

7 No. of artworks
   • quarter-page _____ ; line ____ ; tone ____ ; colours ____
   • half-page   _____ ; line ____ ; tone ____ ; colours ____
   • full-page   _____ ; line ____ ; tone ____ ; colours ____
   • other: _____

8 Production route
   • setting: from disk/manuscript; in-house/typesetter
   • composition: printer/DTP
   • text proof stages: galleys/pages/revises/CRC/film
   • illustration proof stages: scatter/imposed on page

9 Schedule
   • specimen pages needed by _____
   • handover of edited manuscript/disks _____ with/without keyed
     illustrations
   • artwork: briefs to designer   _____ ; roughs   _____ ;
                     roughs approved   _____ ; a/w in   _____
   • commissioned photography: briefs to designer _____
   • marked galleys and all keyed illustrations to design _____
   • layouts/pages to editor _____
   • amended layouts/pages to design _____ with/without index

Figure 6.1 A design brief

Format and filling

Of course, designers need to know the size and shape of the page and any special visual approach that influences those choices, such as detailed cross-sectional artwork or pop-up or sliding features. Share relevant information about the competition that has affected your decisions too. Consulting designers at the proposal stage can give you the benefit of their visual perceptions in defining the specifications. Do not be passive and allow this opportunity to slip by: ask for the designers' views.

Will the estimated number of words, illustrations and pages combine to produce the result you want? It is easy for you to work out the average number of illustrations on a page and their proportionate size when they are going to be in separate plate sections, and even to calculate the probable extent of solid text. However, if the illustrations and text are to be integrated, the spatial relationship between them is an important factor, and designers are trained to manipulate these elements to produce diverse effects. So much depends on what you tell them. It could be disastrous to state the number of words and pictures and ask simply 'Will they fit into that many pages?' Five hundred illustrations and 200 000 words *can* fit into 256 pages, but an affirmative response to your question might not include the enlightening stipulation that the images would be the size of postage stamps and the text would be 8 pt solid type. However, when you add to the bare numerical facts the *effect* that you envisage, designers can begin to assess how to realize that vision.

Part of the effect will be created by the amount of colour — from one to four — and whether it is available in parts of the book or throughout, and whether the illustrations bleed. Thus informed, designers could, for example, advise you on what proportion of the illustrations would be, say, quarter-page, half-page or full-page, and the average number on a spread to get a particular 'look', and they might sketch a few miniature spreads so that together you can fine-tune the image. The style of binding can influence the size of the gutter, and therefore the proportions of the margins generally, and the desirability of running illustrations across spreads. Based on this shared vision, your colleagues can calculate the maximum number of words and illustrations for the given extent, or the extent necessary to contain the numbers originally suggested. Remember to discuss the number of pages needed for prelims and endmatter if they are not included in your word count.

The vision is still an outline; it needs more detail. Discuss with designers what you are trying to achieve and describe your own view, but make it clear that you want their contribution. For example, do you see this book as entirely spread-by-spread or continuous or does some material suggest one style and the rest the other? Perhaps the book will be divided into parts that perform different functions, or organized in chapters only, but they contain regular features, such as summaries, case studies, project work or demonstrations of techniques. The pages will not come to life until designers know how many levels of heading are needed and the range of textual matter, which could include:

- correspondence
- drama
- epigraphs
- extracts
- footnotes or endnotes
- formulae
- lists
- tables
- verse

Listen to, look at and comment on what is being offered until you are convinced that this cross-fertilization of ideas satisfies the readers' needs from the verbal and visual perspectives.

To confirm budgets and schedules, and to plan their work with as much care as you plan yours, designers need to know more about the illustrations than just the total number. Initially, estimate how many of that total are artwork and how many photographs. Then break down the artwork into line and tone, size and colour. Perhaps at the proposal stage you can give only the most general information, such as that there will be 40 two-colour line diagrams averaging a half-page each or 35 full-page tone artworks. Designers will get more detail, of course, when the artwork is being briefed, but they will expect it to fall into the categories quoted. At the earliest point when you see a deviation from this agreed specification, discuss it with them so that they are prepared and can advise you on how the schedule or budget might be affected.

How many, if any, of the photographs are to be commissioned? The difference in cost between colour and black-and-white might be insignificant, but there are other factors that are relevant to time and money. The subject matter may, for example,

- determine or allow a choice of studio or location shots,
- require models, stylists, technicians, supplies and equipment,
- have to be done in particular seasons.

This way or that?

Unless all the books in your house follow the same production route, the decision on the most appropriate route for projects should be the product of consultation with designers and production controllers. All parties need to agree on the proof stages for text and illustrations so that costs and schedules are based on the same information. For books that will be produced from author-generated disks, you must agree who will input editorial changes and code and tag the disks, who will input text changes and corrections at page. Design and production staff will work out where the typesetting and page composition will be done, and will complete that part of the scheduling information.

Artwork

Briefing

Although designers commission the illustrators, you still have to provide the detailed briefs (see Figure 6.2). Because the briefs are to be read by the illustrators, they repeat the general information about the project. Illustrators will use the combination of the age group and knowledge level to inform the degree of detail and sophistication appropriate to the images. It is not enough to tell them that a book is a co-edition; they need to know the implications for the artwork, which may depend on the countries in which the book will be published. For example, there might be objects that must not be represented or that must be represented in particular ways. If illustrators are new to an established series, the quickest way to communicate the style to them is to give them copies of published books. The schedule should include dates when the roughs are due and, just as important, when they will be approved or returned with corrections.

Provide designers with a categorized list of the illustrations: For example:

- 15 line diagrams: 10 quarter-page, 5 half-page, all two-colour,
- 12 tone maps: 8 half-page, 4 full-page, all four-colour,
- 6 tone charts, half-page, four-colour,
- 6 line graphs, quarter-page, two-colour,
- 6 tone cross-sections, double-page spreads, four-colour.

They can quickly see how many and what kinds of illustrator are required. Then group the briefs by the greatest number of common features so that you do not have to repeat information unnecessarily. For example, one group might contain images that will be two-colour line portrait with rules, but with varying reproduction sizes, while another is four-colour tone portrait with rules and varying reproduction sizes. Similarly, each illustration would need its own list of labels, but the remaining points shown in Figure 6.2 would apply to all annotations.

Obviously, the subject is the unique part of the illustration. If the author has provided roughs, make sure they are clear before you pass them on. Not all illustrations require a rough or a reference. Use your common sense to decide which do, and if you are in the slightest doubt, ask the designer or illustrator. Note down on the brief

Project information

1 Subject of the book _____

2 Market
   • age range _____
   • knowledge level _____
   • requirements for intended sales areas _____

3 Series style: examples attached ·

4 Schedule
   • roughs   _____
   • finished artwork   _____

Picture information

1 Subject _____
   • essential content _____
   • essential omissions _____

2 Presentation
   • format: landscape/portrait/square
   • style: squared with rules/squared without rules/
     vignetted/silhouetted/bleeding;
     cartoon/representational/abstract
   • reproduction size _____ × _____
   • line/tone
   • colour: 1/2/3/4

3 Annotations
   • typed and marked-up list attached
   • to be on separate overlay
   • lines/arrows to subject
   • black only/2nd colour/reverse out
   • special requirements for type _____

Figure 6.2 An artwork brief

what has been supplied. When describing what is to be drawn, include everything that must be in the picture and be explicit about what must not be shown and what can be left to the illustrator's discretion. The first step in protecting the project against the danger of authors changing their mind about the content of illustrations after the artwork has been done is to have them confirm the briefs.

Checking

Depending on the complexity of the subject, illustrators' roughs might be submitted for checking before the artwork is finalized. Make sure that you and the authors look at them in detail, because this is the only opportunity to make changes without extra cost. If changes are required, make sure you know whether it is because the briefs were ambiguous or incomplete, the illustrators did not follow the briefs or the authors have changed their mind. Thus you can learn to improve your briefs, provide feedback to illustrators about reading the briefs and remind authors that while minor alterations are usually free, major changes at this stage *might* cost, and any changes to the finished artwork *will* be charged.

Check finished artwork thoroughly against the brief, making sure that alterations asked for at the preliminary stage have been made and no new errors introduced. Proofread the annotations and check style and position. Designers will verify the quality of the work and the suitability of the presentation, but if you have a question, a doubt or a concern, don't be mute: ask them about it.

Photography

Briefing

In some ways briefing photography is like briefing artwork. The purpose is to produce unique images, and as editor you are responsible for stating the essential content and the essential omissions in the briefs. However, there are usually no references to help you visualize the outcome, and no artist's roughs on which you can make alterations.

You and the designers should discuss the general look or style desired so that the designers can select an appropriate photographer. While you need to think very carefully about what you want each image to show and, especially, not show, remember that photography is a creative art. Inessential details in the briefs can, by obstructing the photographer's involvement, preclude the very result you want. To achieve your end, do not prepare and hand over briefs in a rush. Schedule this task so that after you write the briefs, you can put them aside for a day or so and then review them with fresh eyes. Try to see what the photographer will see; is anything important not in the picture, or anything trivial apparent? Discuss the briefs with the designers; does their image match yours? In this way designers can help you, and you can help yourself, to improve your briefing technique.

The designers will brief the photographer on style and format, but if the photographs are to be of objects in public places — for example, buildings, cars, plants or animals — or the locations themselves, no one from the publishing house accompanies the photographer on the shoot. When models are used or objects have to be created or specially arranged — as is the case for craft books, recipe books and science projects in textbooks — designers brief the stylists too and usually go on the shoot for at least part of the time. Editors are invited *sometimes*, but even when you are present, your main contribution has already been made.

Checking

When the photographs arrive, designers will check them for quality. You should mention any worries you have in this respect, but your main job is to look at them for content and visual impact. The content should, of course, be consistent with the brief. If something is missing or unexpectedly present, decide whether it warrants retaking the picture:

- Does it alter the authors' message?
- Does it have the potential to mislead or harm readers, for example, by showing a dangerous way to conduct an experiment, rewire electrical appliances or hold a tool?
- Will it affect sales of the book?

If the answer to any of these questions is yes, the picture must be replaced. When the fault lies in the brief, retakes, which are not budgeted for, will cost as much as the originals and might present scheduling problems. This is an expensive and distressing way to learn to improve your briefing technique. If the answer to any of these questions is no, then do not ask for retakes even if the photographer is responsible for the error. You will not incur any direct financial expense, but there could still be scheduling problems, and it can only impair your professional credibility to demand work that everyone knows is unnecessary.

Covers and jackets

Only a minority of the vast number of titles published is reviewed, and a smaller minority sold on the basis of reviews alone. For the majority, including those that are the subject of publicity campaigns, jackets and covers are used to attract readers and sell the product. Every element on the jacket contributes to this purpose, and every space should be used for it.

Briefing

Give designers who are not working on the content of the book the basic background information:

- subject,
- approach,
- main selling points,
- intended audience,
- markets (domestic or co-edition; trade, direct mail, educational),
- trimmed page size,
- spine width (ask production),
- relevant visual material,
- number of colours and illustrations that the budget allows,
- any restrictions on or demands for the use of particular colours or materials.

Figure 6.3 is a checklist for the editorial information that might be included. Obviously, not all of it is relevant to every book, and individual publishers may put some details in different locations. Covers and jackets are sales and marketing tools, so discuss the relative importance of the elements and the overall look with those colleagues first (see Chapter 11). Then, incorporating their perspective, discuss the brief with designers. Tell them which details are most important and what each part needs to achieve. Perhaps the illustration must catch the eye but the title should hold the attention, and while the author is not yet the main selling point, his or her name must be sufficiently prominent that readers will be aware of it; maybe next time the author's name will be larger, and the time after that be more important than the title and illustration. Whether or not there is an illustration, what is the desired visual impact? Look for combinations of words to convey a visual image — bold, gory, delicate, subtle, colourful, crowded, austere, opulent, authoritative, professional, humorous, friendly, outrageous — and ask designers for feedback on how they are *seeing* what you are saying. When you are sure that you share an understanding of what has to be achieved, the resultant design is very likely to satisfy the committee that has to approve it.

Always ask for at least two, and preferably three, preliminary designs. You may have to use all your persuasive powers here. Many designers dislike providing more than one visual, even though in devising that one they may have discarded two or three others. It is not because of the work involved, but because they want to give you the one they think is best — and from a pure design point of view it might be.

Front
- series title _____
- volume title _____
- volume subtitle _____
- volume number _____
- author/editor _____
- translator _____
- illustrator _____
- edition: new/revised/no. _____
- sales flash _____
- other _____
- no. of illustrations attached _____/to come _____

Spine
- series title _____
- volume title _____
- volume subtitle _____
- volume number _____
- author/editor _____
- illustrator (if joint author) _____
- edition: new/revised/no. _____
- publisher: _____/logo or colophon attached

Back printed cover
- blurb attached
- no. of illustrations attached _____/to come _____
- price _____
- ISBN and bar code attached/to come
- publisher: _____/logo or colophon attached
- country where jacket is printed _____
- credits for design and illustration _____
  _____

Back jacket
- blurb attached
- no. of illustrations attached _____/to come _____
- ISBN and bar code attached/to come
- publisher: _____/logo or colophon attached

Front flap
- blurb attached
- price _____
- illustration caption/credit _____
  _____

Back flap
- author blurb attached
- design credit _____
- publisher: _____/logo or colophon attached
- country where jacket is printed _____

Figure 6.3 Cover and jacket brief

But the people who have to approve it are looking at it from editorial, sales, marketing and production perspectives. It is exceedingly rare that a committee shown only one design will approve it; usually everybody finds fault with something — loss of objectivity is common — and the design is rejected. However, given a choice of several designs, the committee usually agrees on one, sometimes with only minor adjustments, and, yes, it is often the one the designer chose.

Handing over manuscripts, disks and illustrations

It is the simplest and most obvious points that are so often overlooked.

- Make sure manuscripts are complete (remember the prelims), in order and properly marked-up.
- Label disks with the book title, files and software program.
- Number and pack illustrations (see also Chapter 7).
- List everything you are handing over, with dates for any material still to come, and keep a copy of the dated memo or handover form (see Figure 3.1, on pages 40–41).
- Deliver everything together, numbering envelopes or boxes to indicate which one they are of the total: for example, 1/3, 2/3, 3/3.
- Do it on time and confirm the schedule for the next stage.

Do not wait for people to tell you they have a problem. When the designers have had time to look through all the materials, check that they have everything they need and understand your brief.

Maintaining schedules

Your global schedule should show the times you have earmarked for preparing briefs, checking preliminary artwork and checking final artwork and photographs. It signals when you need to arrange briefing and handover meetings, and indicates with whom you must discuss potential delays to any of these procedures.

Designers must be consulted about the time allotted to them in the schedule for all projects, which means asking them to consider in detail and with knowledge of the nature of the project whether the time is adequate to produce the required quality of work. Figure 6.1 shows key stages that may need to be negotiated before the schedule is finalized. When designers have agreed to dates, they are responsible for maintaining them.

To be effectively in control of your job, sustain your dialogue with designers throughout the process, as you do with authors. After briefing and handing over materials, check that designers have all the elements and details they require and still agree with the schedule. If the design phase is a long one, inquire intermittently how the work is going. You might ask about specific problems that had to be addressed, check again that the designers do not need additional materials or information from you or the authors, or just express a general interest; you will, of course, confirm that the designers, and the illustrators and photographers they have commissioned, will be meeting the next scheduled date. This should ensure that you learn of potential delays either because you have asked or because you have established such good relationships with designers that they tell you at the earliest opportunity, before you ask. Then you are in a position to inform others and take action to prevent the delay becoming a crisis.

Maintaining budgets

Designers can estimate costs only when they are briefed. The more accurate your brief, the more accurate the budget is likely to be. Designers are responsible for handling their budgets, but you are responsible for maintaining them by sticking to the original briefs and specifications. You cannot ask for more or more complex illustrations, for commissioned photographs instead of artwork, for more colour or a different format or extent, for a jacket instead of a cover, or for editorial changes that are not essential without having an impact on the budget and possibly the schedule. None the less, there are times when you or the designers might think such changes are necessary or desirable. In those cases, discuss the reasons for the suggested changes — do they make the book more saleable? — and ask the designers to assess the implications for the budget and schedule. Perhaps together you can find other, less disruptive ways of achieving the same end or see that the result will not be worth the cost. On those rare occasions when you are ready to agree to alterations that increase design costs, consider in what other areas you can make savings to maintain the project budget and discuss the possibilities with the colleagues concerned.

Checking page layouts

Your objective is to make sure that the pages are complete, continuous, consistent, balanced and obey the conventions, individually and collectively.

1 *Complete* Ascertain that all the pages, from prelims to endmatter, are present, and that everything intended is on each page: text, captions, tables, running heads, folios, footnotes, illustrations.

2 *Continuous* Scan the text to see that it runs from line to line and page to page with no dropped or repeated matter. As discrete tasks, check that the pages run in numerical sequence, that the appropriate running heads are on each page and that illustrations and tables are numbered or lettered sequentially. It is difficult to do these jobs efficiently if you are looking at other details at the same time.

3 *Consistent* Look at the spacing between the various elements, such as the top of the text area and the chapter heading, the chapter heading and the first line of text, text and illustrations, illustrations and captions, captions and text, text and footnotes. *Measure* only when there is a jarring optical inconsistency.

Make certain that the rules governing the use of rectos or versos for chapter openers, the position of folios and the omission of running heads on chapter openers, the measure and position of captions in relation to illustrations, the position of numerals or letters to identify multiple illustrations covered by a block caption, and the balancing of columns are clear and consistently imposed.

Check that textual references and captions correspond to the illustrations, that sequential illustrations are always placed in the same order, and that system of identifying illustrations by numerals or letters is consistently imposed.

4 *Balanced* See that the illustrations and text on each page are visually accessible, and that the number, size and distribution of illustrations throughout the extent is balanced without being boring.

5 *Conventions* Ensure that headings at the bottom of the page have at least two, but preferably three, lines of text under them, and adjust widows and orphans, and word-breaks at the bottom of rectos, or at the bottom of all columns and pages, depending on the nature of the book and the needs of the targeted reader.

Cut overmatter or fill columns or pages where necessary, working from the end of paragraphs. Common sense tells you to look for widows or short lines when there are only a few lines to be cut, and to look for blocks of text when there are many. Similarly, look for long lines at the end of paragraphs that need only a few words to create a new line. If you have tried and failed to cut or fill, as a *last resort* ask designers if they can adjust the type on computer.

Check that illustrations are placed as close to the text reference as possible. If they cannot be on the same page as the reference in the text, they should be on a following, not preceding, page.

Alterations

When a layout does not seem to work, pinpoint the reasons. For example:

- Is text squashed between illustrations or vice versa?
- Does the position of an image or the arrangement of a spread pull the reader's eyes towards the gutter or edge of the page?
- Does the arrangement of one page conflict with that of the facing page?
- Are important details in an illustration that goes across a spread lost in the gutter?
- Is the spacing between elements too little or too great for the reader to make essential connections easily?

Be sure to consider each spread on its own and as part of the chapter and the book. Sometimes a layout does not work because it is stylistically inconsistent with other pages; sometimes breaking the grid or format at intervals enlivens the book visually. Remember not to let your personal taste affect your judgement and do not worry about consistency for its own sake; always consider the visual effect in terms of its impact on the message and the audience.

When you have assessed the nature of the problem, see if you can think of solutions that are practical: cost-effective, quick and without negative knock-on effects. Remember to explain problems to designers, as you do to authors, in objective terms: 'the layout doesn't seem to work for the reader because …', 'the illustration seems to pull the reader's eye …', 'the position of the captions might confuse …'. Offer your *suggestions* — 'I thought maybe', 'I wonder if', 'Maybe we could' — to designers to evaluate along with their own ideas or, if you cannot see the solutions, ask them to explain to you what can be done. Be sure to invite discussion of possible effects on pages not directly concerned as well as those at issue. Use these opportunities to learn. Do not accept changes until you understand them. It is not important who suggests the ultimate solution; it is important that you agree that the solution is the best one for the book and the reader.

Colour proofs

Colour illustrations can be proofed on proofing presses, photographically or digitally. Editors and designers rarely have differences of opinion when they are checking that illustrations have been accurately sized and cropped, and marking obvious blemishes, such as scratches, blotches and specks of dirt, for correction. It is attitudes to colour itself that can cause strained relations.

You and the designers will compare the original and the proof. In most circumstances you would like the colours in the proofs to be the same as those in the originals. You are expected to mark for correction colours that are wrong — blue instead of green, red instead of brown, yellow instead of orange — or too dark or too light, or out of register. As long as no one is colourblind, you and the designers are still in agreement. However, harmony and understanding are seriously at risk if you try to mark proofs to reflect every nuance of colour in every illustration. In the first place, marking percentage colour changes is a skilled job, and guesswork can lead to self-contradictory muddles. In the second place, designers and production controllers can explain to you why reproduction is not 100% accurate; it might be the nature, number and quality of the originals, the limitations of the four-colour process, or the quality of origination, paper and printing that the budget allows.

Rather than scrutinizing the proof for every variation from the original, consider what the readers expect. For example, people buying a very inexpensive book do not expect the illustrations to be of the same quality as in an expensive book. They will see only the printed version, not the original artwork or photographs, which, in any case, might not faithfully reproduce the colours in their subjects. Look at the proofs again and decide if the slight alterations you want to make to the colour are important to the authors' message, the readers' understanding or the saleability of the book.

In that small proportion of cases where you decide the changes do make an important difference, explain to the designer how you think the colours should appear and why, and ask what effect the changes would have on the particular illustrations and on others. For example, let us say you want to change the shade of green in a number of illustrations and increase the red in others. The designer might tell you that increasing the yellow by a specific percentage will produce the desired green, but it will make the red more orange and the violet, which you had not even considered, appear purple. Discussing the options together, you might compromise on increasing the yellow to improve the green a little without damaging the red and violet noticeably. Remember that these discussion, as well as the changes, take time and therefore cost money; make sure they are important.

7
Working with picture researchers

Picture researcher is a slight misnomer, for these people do not research pictures, but search for photographs. They also do a lot more than that, and to work with them effectively, you must understand the scope of their job and your part in it.

Snapshot

Some picture researchers are generalists, who enjoy the challenge of looking for photos on all subjects; others are specialists, with knowledge of and interest in a particular field; some work in-house, the majority are freelance. Their main job, from which all their other tasks derive, is to obtain existing photographs for reproduction. Depending on the subjects, the sources might be museums, galleries, picture libraries and agencies, private collectors, manufacturers, tourist agencies, government departments, consulates, film companies, magazines and newspapers, academic archives or scientific research organizations. Picture researchers will visit some local sources and will travel when requested to do so, but they will also do their work by telephone, fax, e-mail and letter.

When photographs arrive, picture researchers will check that they correspond to the source's delivery note and that they are in good physical condition, reporting discrepancies in the list or damage to the photographs to the source immediately. Each time they return photographs (see 'Schedules and procedures', below), picture researchers will pack and send them to ensure their safe delivery in good condition, and include a list of what the package contains. Picture researchers also negotiate the terms and conditions for use — that is, they clear permissions and negotiate fees — and prepare the acknowledgements that will be printed in the book. They are responsible for keeping clear documentation of all these processes and, if they are freelance, for handing it over at the end of the job.

Researchers can be asked to acquire information about photographs from the sources, but they are not expected to write captions. They do not look for references for artwork, and although some picture researchers commission photography, in book publishing this is usually the preserve of the designer (see Chapter 6).

Briefing

Picture researchers are part of the team that produces an illustrated book, and, where feasible, they should be briefed at an early stage with their colleagues, which saves time in clarifying the basic issues, allows researchers to contribute to the exchange of ideas that produces the best books, and promotes teamwork. Figure 7.1 is an outline of the written part of the brief, which is discussed in detail below. In-house researchers should, of course, be consulted about their part of the budget and schedule when you are preparing a publishing proposal.

Project basics

Whether they are briefed sooner or later, are in-house or, as is more common, free-lance, all picture researchers need the same general information about the project in order to do their job.

---

1 Subject

2 Intended market
   - age range
   - knowledge level

3 Markets
   - domestic or countries of co-edition
   - educational or trade

4 Specifications
   - format
   - extent
   - number of words
   - number of illustrations in total and ratio to text
   - number of photographs in colour/black-and-white
   - copy of previous books in series, specimen pages or flat-plan

5 Detailed picture list

6 Copy of the manuscript when available

7 Schedule

8 Budget

9 Statement of responsibilities, for freelancers

Figure 7.1 Information to include in a picture research brief

1 *Subject* Obviously, picture researchers need to know what they are looking for. The subject of the book gives them the first indication of the visual images that are their goal and, therefore, a preliminary idea of the most appropriate places to look for them. This, in turn, supplies some of the information needed to estimate the costs and time involved.

2 *Intended audience* The readers' age range and experience provides clues as to how general or specialized, common or rare the pictures might have to be, and thus can help researchers refine their choice of potential sources and give them a clearer idea of schedules and budgets.

3 *Markets* Depending on the subject matter, whether a book is for a domestic or international audience might influence the types of illustration needed and the sources that have to be approached. In addition, the fees that researchers have to negotiate for reproducing photographs are based partly on the amount of exposure that the images will get. Exposure is evaluated by the size at which the photograph will be reproduced, the number of copies of the book that will be published and the number of countries in which it will be published. Most sources have discounted rates for schoolbooks, encyclopedias and manuals.

4 *Specifications* Combining these elements in a variety of ways, picture researchers can extract more information to add to what they already know:

- the number of photographs = the size of the job, and therefore the amount of time it might take,
- the number of photographs and the proportion in colour = sources and costs,
- the number of illustrations and the ratio to words = average reproduction size of images, which affects costs,
- the number of illustrations, the proportion in colour, the ratio to words, the page size and the estimated selling price = quality, which influences choice of sources, time and costs.

Although we are concerned with conventional book publishing, you should also specify if the book will be available in electronic form, as there will be separate fees. Previous books in the series, specimen pages or flat-plans are visual aids that can help picture researchers more accurately assess the job and carry out the work.

In-house picture researchers should have this information as soon as the proposal is approved or the team is assembled. You would need to give the same information, plus the outline schedule (see 'Schedules and procedures', below), verbally to freelancers well before the work is to start to see if they are available and interested (see also Chapter 9). When the full briefing takes place, this information should be typed and dated.

Picture details

The picture list is the blueprint of the researchers' job. As a working document it needs to be a self-contained part of the full brief, each page numbered and dated (see 'Making changes', below). Be as sure as possible that the list is complete when you hand it over. Picture researchers expect to bring in an assortment of images for each subject and they allow time to return those not selected or to continue to search for better alternatives, but it is a waste of money and their time and effort if subjects are deleted from the list after they have taken steps to obtain them. Similarly, adding new subjects at a late stage may mean that picture researchers have to revisit sources, in person or in writing, for photographs they could easily have procured the first time. Although it sometimes proves necessary to alter information on picture lists, you should assess and plan the job to keep changes to an absolute minimum, even delaying the starting date if you are aware of the possibility of a large number of changes.

The amount of detail you provide for each subject should help picture researchers to find the image you need. If you give too little, they might waste their time looking in the wrong places or getting the wrong picture; if you give too much, you might restrict their contribution and limit the possibility of useful alternatives. As for artwork and commissioned photography, the brief should state essential content and essential omissions. For example, if the subject is a specific work of art, the basic information would be:

- the type of work, including the medium when it is known that the artist worked on the same subject in more than one; for example, oil painting, watercolour, clay model, stone/marble/bronze sculpture, tapestry, mobile and so on,
- the title,
- the date if there is more than one work by that title,
- name of the artist,
- location of the work if known.

Let us suppose that the subject is less well defined: any type of work by a particular artist. Then the most useful information would be:

- the name of the artist,
- the media in which he or she worked,
- the location(s) of major collections of his or her work.

You can modify these details to show that the subject is any example of one type of work by that artist, or any example of a particular type of work by one of several artists.

In addition, there might be some elements that are desirable — wanted if the choice is readily available — but not essential. For example, there can be different views of a three-dimensional object. Works that are photographed indoors are likely to show the front, sides and back, but objects outdoors can also be shot from above, from the ground looking up, at different times of day and in different seasons. Photographs of large buildings might not be able to encompass the entire edifice, might show some details and not others, might include people or passing traffic. State clearly on the list which of these elements are vital and which are preferred, and do not mention the others.

Apply the same kind of analysis to determine what information to provide for each subject. Thus, when the subjects are people, you might consider whether it is essential or preferred that they are seen

- alone or in a group,
- posed or in natural circumstances,
- dressed formally or casually,
- in a particular place,
- in whole or in part, from the front, back or side,
- on a particular occasion or in a particular year.

Some of this information might be stated as essential omissions: the photograph must not show the subject with a named individual, or engaging in a certain activity, or in uniform, or at a particular place, or before or after a designated date.

Often, authors will have seen a photograph of the subject they want to illustrate and will produce a photocopy or the name of the source in which they have seen it. This can be helpful if that photograph is the only existing or appropriate one of the subject, or if it is intended to identify a very unusual object. Otherwise, asking for that same picture to be supplied can needlessly restrict choice. For example, events — a battle, an election campaign, a sports tournament — can take place over a period of time and over a large area and involve many people. Even those that are very limited in time, place and participants can be seen from different angles. To insist on a single image because it is the only one the authors have seen is to preclude the possibility of getting an equally good, or better, shot, and perhaps one that has not been published as often or at all.

As well as the editorial content, the list must state the requirements for colour and format. When the specification is the same for all subjects, it can be given as a general instruction. That can include saying that the format does not matter and that all photographs should be in colour where there is a choice. Otherwise, colour or black-and-white, portrait or landscape should be specified for each subject.

Images for the jacket and the blad, if you are producing one, need to be available before those for the rest of the book (see 'Schedules and procedures', below). However, the subjects are not always chosen before picture research begins, so warn picture researchers of when this decision will be made and the approximate number of photographs that will be affected.

Putting researchers in the picture

A list of subjects does not make the brief complete. As well as visual materials, picture researchers should be given a copy of the manuscript. They do not need the edited version, but it helps, especially in a long text, if you highlight the passages to which the illustrations relate. Referring to the text can give picture researchers more information about what has been requested or what alternatives they can suggest.

The written brief, which must contain details of the schedule and budget, and, for freelancers, a statement of their responsibilities to the company and the company's responsibilities to them, is, of course, a starting point (see below and Figure 7.2). The real briefing occurs when you and the picture researchers discuss all the major points. Picture researchers may elicit from you details you had not realized would be useful to them or ask you to clarify ambiguities. They might explain to you that some items on the list are impossible because they predate the invention of the camera, that others are not available in colour at all or only after a certain date, or that they know of alternatives you might want to consider. They might point out that some pictures have to come from sources that are very slow to deliver, have stringent conditions or require prepayment. Depending on the length and complexity of the list, picture researchers might want to take time to assess the job in detail before confirming the dates or the costs, or that they have all the information they need.

Schedules and procedures

You have sketched in the following dates on your global schedule, and you should agree them with the picture researchers at the appropriate time. Here is what happens at each stage.

Book

1 *Full briefing* Arrange a meeting at which you will hand over the complete picture list and discuss the project.
2 *Preliminary selection* Arrange another meeting. Picture researchers will bring you the photographs they have obtained, minus the ones they have rejected because

they did not fulfil the editorial requirements or because they were of poor repro-
ductive quality. At this time you, the picture researchers, authors and designers
decide which of the remaining images should be retained for possible use. Picture
researchers will return the rejects to their sources. The date should be:

- long enough after the full briefing to get in the majority of subjects,
- soon enough to allow returns to be made without incurring holding fees,
- long enough before the final selection to allow time to fill gaps or to obtain
  the originals when only duplicates have been seen.

Throughout this and other selection processes, picture researchers will keep
you informed of any special terms and conditions attached to the photographs,
such as restrictions on cropping, model releases required or the need to submit
colour proofs for approval.

3 *Final selection* Another misnomer. This is the date by which you need to have all
   the originals in-house in order to allow time to select the subjects that will be
   illustrated. There may be some rejects during this process, but designers might
   also want to retain a number of photographs for individual subjects to allow
   them flexibility in laying out the pages. It is vital that you keep picture
   researchers informed of these decisions and let them have the final rejects as soon
   as possible so that they can negotiate the time with, and return the unused illustrations to, the sources without incurring loan fees.

4 *Page layouts* Now that the final selection has been made, picture researchers can
   return all photographs not being used to their sources and prepare the picture
   credits to be printed in the book. They will notify sources whose photographs are
   being used of the size of reproduction, the date of publication, the market rights
   required and the published title, so that the sources can send in their invoices.

5 *Bound copies* The photographs will be back from the origination house. Picture
   researchers will check that all the images have been returned in good condition
   and in the right mount, then return them to the sources. They might also have to
   negotiate additional fees if the pictures have been used for publicity. Picture
   researchers are expected to check that invoices correspond to the terms they
   negotiated. Many publishers also like picture researchers to mark up a file copy
   of the book, writing the sources on the page with the illustration.

6 *Publication* This is the date when invoices are paid. Freelance picture researchers
   should hand over all the documents relating to the project.

Jackets and blads

The dates for producing jackets and blads (see Chapter 11) are a separate line on
your global schedule and create mini-schedules for picture researchers. You might
not have included a preliminary selection date for the illustration(s) for the jacket or

This confirms our agreement to engage you as Picture Researcher on the title named in the attached specification. You agree to:

1 Provide sufficient photographs of the subjects on the attached list for selection in accordance with the specification and schedule, and of good quality for reproduction

2 Get, wherever possible, good illustrations that have not been often published

3 Provide, wherever possible, information for captioning purposes from the sources

4 Clear copyright and negotiate reproduction fees for the markets and within the budget stated

5 Check all delivery notes for accuracy, log incoming and outgoing materials to ensure that you know where/with whom materials for which you are responsible are at all times

6 Check all incoming materials for condition and inform sources of materials that are received damaged

7 Ensure that no holding fees are incurred, by arranging that material is returned in time or that an extension to the loan period is requested

8 Return all pictures to source after use accompanied by a detailed delivery note, request invoices to be sent on publication and check invoices for accuracy

9 Ensure that all materials you send from one place to another are properly packaged to prevent them from being damaged

10 Ensure that you send all materials by the safest means possible

11 Accept responsibility, and pay loss or damage fees, for materials in your possession

12 Provide a complete and accurate list of Picture Credits in the form agreed with the editor, and to mark up a file copy of the book

13 To liaise with the editor as required, especially to ensure that she or he is immediately informed of any problems that might affect the schedule, budget, choice or quality of illustrations

14 Keep complete and accurate documentation for all picture research and hand it over to the company at the end of the project

15 Supply necessary receipts and records of cost for expenses, such as postage, telephone and travel

Figure 7.2 A picture research contract

The company agrees to

1   Provide a clear and comprehensive brief of the illustrations required

2   Provide a copy of the manuscript when possible and if necessary

3   Provide a letter of authorization to sources when requested

4   Provide company stationery as required

5   Assume responsibility for the condition of photographs in the possession of its staff, reproduction house, printer, or other subcontractor until they are returned to the picture researcher, and pay loss or damage fees incurred by any of these parties

6   Abide by the terms and conditions stipulated by the sources and to pay their invoices on publication

7   Pay you _____ and reimburse you for expenses to a maximum of _____

8   Pay you for work done and reimburse you for expenses incurred for ·obtaining and returning all pictures to their sources if the project should be cancelled after signature of this contract, and negotiate suitable compensation

To confirm your acceptance of these terms and conditions, please sign one copy of this contract and return it to us keeping the other copy.

for the company

_____   _____

Date _____   Date _____

---

cover, which might be independent of the pictures that will be used in the book, but if you have, the final selection date will not be long afterwards. If you are producing a blad, the illustration(s) for the front of the jacket will be used on it. The pictures for inside the blad must be ones that will be used in the book, but their selection dates will be the same as those for the jacket. Picture researchers can return jacket illustrations that definitely will not be used inside the book to their sources after all the jackets are printed; those for the blad after the book is printed.

Speed can be expensive

Naturally, you will ask picture researchers to consider all aspects of the schedule carefully, and to warn you at the earliest moment of potential delays. They will be responsible for meeting dates to which they have agreed, and will negotiate with sources for timely deliveries. Sometimes picture researchers will consult you to see how important a particular picture is to determine whether it is worth paying a premium to get it on time. The premium may be a higher fee to a normally slow source or the cost of special delivery or courier services if the schedule is tight and the source is distant. If your schedules are always tight or if you add new subjects at a late stage, the budget is bound to be affected and so are your relationships with picture researchers.

There may be times — it could be at the briefing or when they locate an illustration — when picture researchers inform you that a source takes more time than you have available and cannot be influenced to move more quickly. Do not expect them to work miracles; some sources set long turn-around times from which they will not deviate. Choose a different subject or discuss with the designer if you can afford to wait for this image.

Budgets

Sources charge for the use of their materials. There are fees for copyright and reproduction permission (see Chapter 10), and there may be separate charges if you use any of the images for blads, catalogues or any other form of advertising. There can be search fees even when picture researchers visit the premises and look through the files themselves. There are print fees for halftones, which means the prints do not have to be returned, although you cannot use them again without getting permission and paying.

Holding fees can be avoided. Sources stipulate how long you can keep colour transparencies for selection purposes. There is usually no charge for pictures you do not want to use that are returned within that period of time. Before that time expires, you should inform picture researchers if the decisions will be delayed so that they can try to negotiate a longer free loan period. There are no holding fees for pictures that are retained for use in the book.

When you employ freelance picture researchers, there must also be a budget for their fee and expenses. Reasonable expenses include transport by the least expensive means feasible (for example, public transport rather than taxis for visiting sources); postage, unless all letters and dispatch of photographs will be sent through the company; telephone and fax. If a project is cancelled for any reason after freelance picture researchers have been employed and started work, they must, of course, be paid for the work they have done and for sending back photographs that have been received. You should also negotiate reasonable compensation because you have reserved their time and they will have turned away other work that they could have done in that period (see also Chapter 9).

Picture researchers are responsible for maintaining the agreed budgets. They will negotiate discounts for bulk purchases and for educational use, look for free sources for some illustrations to offset the cost of commercial ones for others, and keep a running estimate so that they can consult you if there is a danger of going over-budget. Do your part: make sure there is no danger to the budget because of late changes to the brief or greater demands on a freelancer's time.

Making changes

Keep a copy of the typed and dated brief. If you and the picture researchers agree to alter any elements — subjects, specifications, details of the schedule or budget — write the changes on both copies and initial and date them. After that, of course, you will try to alter the brief as little as possible, if at all. But when you have to, try to speak to the picture researcher first. It provides an opportunity to discuss alternatives as well as implications for the schedule and the budget. Even voice-mail is preferable to the unheralded arrival of what, in effect, are new demands.

Following oral contact, send a copy of the original brief with the changes marked on it, initialled and dated. This avoids confusion and precludes arguments: both you and the picture researchers have a record of what was changed and when.

Care and control of photographs

When picture researchers supply photographs to you, they will include a list of what is in the package or, at the very least, the number of halftones and the number of transparencies. You should check, as the picture researchers do, that the pictures match the delivery note and that they are in good physical condition. Immediately inform picture researchers of any discrepancy or damage. Follow the same procedures when photographs are returned to you from design or production.

You are responsible for the photographs while they are in your possession. Sources, even those that might allow you to use the photographs for free, will charge heavily for loss or damage. The rules are simple and obvious, which is probably why they need repeating so often.

1 *Do not mark photographs* Writing on the back of halftones, even with a soft pencil, can break the emulsion on the front and ruin the photographs. Leave it to experienced designers to make any marks on transparencies; even if you have a chinagraph pencil, don't do it.

- To number photographs for keying into the text, write the numbers on self-adhesive labels (not the partially self-adhesive ones that are meant to be removable) and *then* place the labels on the back of halftones or the mount of transparencies, being careful not to cover up any information already there.
- To indicate the area of an image you want reproduced, mark photocopies of halftones or photomechanical enlargements of transparencies, or measure the area, draw it on an overlay, and *then* attach the overlay to the picture so that the tape touches only the back of halftones or the frame of transparencies.

2 *Keep photographs safe in your care*

- Work with photographs on a clean surface from which sharp objects — loose paperclips, staples, scissors, pens — and glasses, cups, jars or bottles containing so much as a drop of liquid have been removed.
- Keep the photographs on the opposite side of your body from the hand holding a pen or pencil.
- Keep photographs away from the edge of the surface so they cannot fall or be knocked off onto the floor or into the wastebasket, where they might be damaged or lost.
- When you are not working on them, stack photographs neatly in a suitable container — a folder, envelope or box — from which they cannot fall out, and put it in a drawer, preferably a metal one, which provides greater protection from fire and sprinkler systems than a wooden one.

3 *Keep photographs safe in transit*

- Pack photographs carefully so that halftones do not bend and the corners of the frames do not stick into other transparencies.
- For internal transmission, to design or production, use folders or envelopes from which the pictures cannot fall out. Mark them with the project title and the number and description of the contents (for example, 34 halftones, or 25 halftones and 10 transparencies for Chapter 2) *before* putting the photographs inside.
- For external transmission, pack the photographs as above in cardboard-backed or padded envelopes. Enclose a letter or memo stating the project title and the number and description of the contents. Mark the envelopes 'Photos: Do Not Bend'. Check the current level of compensation for lost goods, then send the photographs registered, with extra insurance, or by courier, as appropriate.

Picture credits

Picture researchers usually prepare the acknowledgements to sources for permission to use their photographs (see also Chapter 10). They need to know where you intend the credits to appear: in the prelims, as part of the captions, or in the endmatter. There are some sources that insist on being credited on the same page as the illustration appears, although this is the exception rather than the rule in book publishing. If you are including the credit for each photograph in its caption, either on the page on in the prelims, picture researchers will give you the wording to use. If the acknowledgements are to appear en bloc, picture researchers will prepare the typed copy. If there are multiple images on a page, discuss with them how these will be indicated.

8

Working with production

In many publishing environments the editorial relationship with production is marked, and marred, by a lack of communication. The underlying reasons for this have their origins in the historical development of modern publishing and old-fashioned attitudes toward manufacturing versus office work; in a word, snobbery. There is no excuse for such prejudices today. All members of the team contribute special knowledge and skills to the production of the book, and deserve the respect of their colleagues. The way we earn each other's respect, and maximize each individual's contribution to the team effort, is by the exchange of information and ideas. Because as editors you are the initiators of the projects, it is your responsibility to open the channels of communication and keep them flowing. Saying 'good morning' and handing over estimate requests, manuscripts or proofs is not enough; you must ask questions and explicitly invite suggestions and opinions — in other words, you must develop dialogue. To do that and to be an effective editor, whether you are commissioning, managing projects or copy-editing, you must understand how the work you do affects the production processes and is affected by them.

What they do

Production controllers are responsible for the physical qualities of the finished book. 'Production' refers specifically to the manufacturing stages from typesetting to binding, although the work itself is not usually carried out by the production department. The stages shown in Figure 8.1 may vary in detail from firm to firm, and even from title to title, depending on the extent to which a book is illustrated, the size of the firm and who does which jobs, and the technology used. For example, in what is usually referred to as the conventional route, production controllers select typesetters to set text, from manuscripts or disks, and compose pages, although in some houses, it is editors who deal with typesetters, hence their title 'production editor'. In what is commonly known as desktop publishing, however, the keyboarding is begun by the authors, amended by the editors and converted to

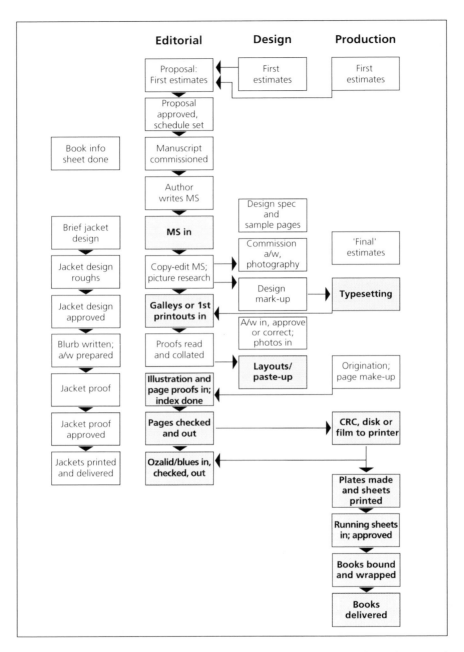

Figure 8.1 The book production processes. The shaded boxes show the critical path. In DTP some stages are combined and may be the responsibility of editorial and design rather than production. The first column shows the preparation of jackets, which go through the same processes as the book itself but on a separate schedule.

type in some houses by the designers and in others by production controllers, who also do the page make-up. Eventually, even the high-resolution origination of illustrations, currently the work of reproduction houses contracted by production departments, will be done in-house. Production controllers, who may or may not be responsible for that in-house development, will still be in charge of specifying paper and other materials, selecting, and negotiating and working with printers, binders and delivery services.

Getting advice

You can learn a great deal about production processes from books and courses, but they may not be available just when you need them, they might not address the specific issues concerning you, or the rapid changes in technology might mean that you need up-to-date information.

At any time in your career, when you are uncertain of your knowledge — especially when you begin to work on a different kind of publication or move from one company to another, where production may be handled differently — discuss the procedures or processes concerned with production controllers. Learn from them not only how to prepare materials in a particular way, but why that way is preferred. When you understand why, it is easy to remember what to do and even to think of other aspects of the work that might be affected. There are many opportunities to learn from production and to invite their help even when you do not have a problem.

Estimate requests

Although production is usually seen as the last stages of bringing a book into existence, it is, of course, involved from the very beginning, when you are preparing the proposal. Chapter 2 pointed out that you have to get estimates of costs from editorial and design colleagues (see Figure 2.4). These are usually so few that forms are unnecessary. However, production includes the cost of transforming the editorial and design elements into a form suitable for manufacturing as well as the cost of materials, the manufacturing itself and delivery from the printer to the warehouse or other destination. Most publishing houses use a production estimate request form to deal with these more numerous costs (see Figure 8.2). (Yes, there really are some houses that operate without such a form, at least until their own inefficiency drives them into creating one or out of business.) It avoids excessive verbiage and lists all the essential elements in the detail necessary, which often reminds you to think about aspects you might have forgotten. Some are

Estimate request form

To _____   From _____

Date _____   Date costing required _____

Series _____

Title _____

Author(s)/Editor _____

Proposed published price _____   Proposed publication date _____

Editorial and design costs

Translation _____   Copy-editing _____   Proofreading _____

Index _____   Text permissions _____   Other fees _____

Picture research _____   Picture fees _____

Book design _____   A/w _____   Jacket/cover design _____

Specification

Trimmed page size _____ × _____ mm/inches

Extent _____ pp total, of which

_____ pp 1/1   Allow _____ pp prelims

_____ pp 4/4   Allow _____ pp endmatter

_____ pp /

Setting

Supplied as hard copy/on author's disk/finished disk

_____ words text, prelims and endmatter   No. of tables _____

_____ words captions   No. of recipes _____

_____ words per full page of text set in 1/2/3 columns

Illustrations

	No. overlays	2-pp	1-p	$\frac{1}{2}$ p	$\frac{1}{3}$ p	$\frac{1}{4}$ p	Total	on disk
transparencies	—	—	—	—	—	—	—	❏
b/w halftones	—	—	—	—	—	—	—	❏
duotones	—	—	—	—	—	—	—	❏
a/w in 4 colours	—	—	—	—	—	—	—	❏
a/w in 2 colours	—	—	—	—	—	—	—	❏
a/w in 1 colour	—	—	—	—	—	—	—	❏
maps in 4 colours	—	—	—	—	—	—	—	❏
maps in 2 colours	—	—	—	—	—	—	—	❏
maps in 1 colour	—	—	—	—	—	—	—	❏

Bleed/no bleed/box rules   No. cutouts __   No. cut-ins __

No. __ tinted panels in ___ colours   Other _____

Figure 8.2 An estimate request form for an illustrated book. Simplified versions can be used for unillustrated books in a range of standard formats.

Endpapers
Plain/printed in __ colours from transparency/halftone/artwork/Pantone colour
same/different subject each end

Jackets
In ___ colours from ___ halftones/transparencies/a/w, with a/w for type
Laminated

Printed laminated covers
in ____ colours from ___ halftones/transparencies/a/w, with a/w for type
Laminated/with foil/emboss

Covers
in ___colours from ___halftones/transparencies/a/w, with a/w for type
Laminated/varnished

Binding
Cased/paperback ☐   Blocking on spine only/spine and front/and jacket
Sewn/unsewn ☐   Head and tail bands ☐   Rounded/flat back ☐
Boxed/slipcase/shrinkwrapped
___ pp plates as wraps/inserts/sections

Print runs/sales

Domestic	cased	plc	p/b	total	
trade	___	___	___	___	
book club	___	___	___	___	
export	___	___	___	___	___

Foreign: separate/run on to domestic edition

	cased	plc	p/b	total	
CIF _____	___	___	___	___	
CIF _____	___	___	___	___	
CIF _____	___	___	___	___	___
					___

Imprint change only/other changes _____

designed to allow for the costs to be estimated on different print runs, but you have to use separate forms to get varying costs on the other elements. For the forms to be useful, you must fill them out completely and clearly. If you do not understand the terminology or the relevance of a category, ask a production controller to explain it to you.

Fixed and variable

Editorial and design costs are fixed: they are not dependent on the number of copies of a single edition. Production costs are both fixed and variable. The fixed costs include:

- typesetting, proofs and proof corrections,
- page make-up to film, proofs and corrections,
- black-and-white reproduction, proofs and corrections,
- colour reproduction, proofs and corrections,
- jacket reproduction, proofs and corrections,
- imprint changes,
- brasses,
- platemaking,
- make ready,
- courier or freight for materials between the house and suppliers prior to manufacture (although sometimes this is treated as an overhead).

Manufacturing costs are determined by the number of copies produced; prices decrease as the print run increases until they reach a minimum. These variable costs include:

- paper: text, ends, plates, jacket,
- covers: paper or boards and cloth or imitation cloth,
- printing,
- binding,
- delivery of books from the manufacturer to the publisher(s).

When you consider the areas for which production controllers are responsible, you begin to understand how they contribute to the way the book looks and how they can help you to achieve your goal. Take paper for example. Production controllers know about the properties and qualities of paper as well as its cost, so they will choose one that is not only suitable for the type of illustrations but also appropriate to the quality required for the intended market. They will consider the whiteness and opacity of the paper, its weight and bulk. The format and extent using a particular paper determines the weight and bulk of the book, and all these characteristics will play a part in decisions that production controllers make about cover materials and binding. The type and number of colour illustrations and the quality you are aiming for will also influence their choice of reproduction house and printer. In addition, they will take into account the format of the book, the size of the print run, the number and location of co-edition partners and the length of the schedule when selecting a printer. Because their decisions are based on combining the specifications in a variety of ways, a change to a single detail — to bleed illustrations, enlarge the format, increase the extent, add foil to the cover — may result in numerous alterations to decisions about materials and suppliers, which can also have repercussions on the budget and schedule.

A form like the one shown in Figure 8.2 is a starting point not only for the estimate but also for dialogue between you and the designer and the production controller. Although as commissioning editor you might have an image of the finished pages, only in developing your vision with the designer will you be able to plan, for example, the number of tinted panels or how and how often box rules will be used. Asking the production controller about the most cost-effective way of creating those panels or box rules might help determine the most appropriate production route for the project. You might not even have considered the endpapers, but the designer might suggest that coloured endpapers would enhance the appearance of the book. Rather than just putting that on the form, ask the production controllers to evaluate the cost differences of using coloured paper or printing in colour. Your chosen format might look great, but ask the production controller if it is economical; perhaps altering it by a fraction will save a lot of money and not make any difference to the overall look. You know about even workings, but do you know the most economical multiples for your chosen format? You can ask the production controller for a list of extents with the 'ideal' ones marked. Explaining the quality level you want to achieve and the market you want to reach can lead to discussions about bulk, bleeds and binding, the relative merits of head and tail bands, and the ramifications of co-editions.

During these conversations you might revise some aspect of your concept, the designer might see another way to achieve that effect and the production controller might suggest how it can be facilitated by a particular imposition. Such discussions and decisions allow production controllers to make more informed choices of paper and other materials, suppliers and printer at an early stage. This can save time and money, and ensure that the finished book matches your expectation and meets the needs of the market.

Figure 8.3 is a typical estimate form for illustrated books. Using the information provided on the estimate request, production controllers work out the fixed and variable (manufacturing) costs. The total cost divided by the print run equals the unit cost — the cost of a single copy (see also Chapter 2).

A reliable result

The first estimate that production controllers give you will be sufficiently accurate for working out the viability of the proposal. It will be based on their experience of other books with similar specifications or a price from one trusted supplier. If the proposed publication date is a long time in the future, a contingency figure for price

First/revised estimate

To _____   From_____

Date _____

Title _____   Format _____

Extent _____

	Quantity	Run on
Fixed costs		
Total editorial		
Total design		
Typesetting		
House corrections @ __ %		
Page composition		
House corrections @ __ %		
B/w reproduction		
Colour reproduction		
Cover/jacket reproduction and bulk proofs		
Brass		
Prepress transport		
Total fixed		
Manufacturing costs		
Paper		
Cover paper		
Jacket paper		
Boards		
Foil		
Extras		
Make ready		
Printing: text		
plate change		
colour plates		
cover/jacket		
Binding		
Transport		
Storage		
Contingency @ __ %		
Total manufacturing		
Total cost		
Unit cost		

Figure 8.3 A production estimate form

changes may have to be incorporated. There is no point in getting competitive prices from a number of suppliers at this stage because the controllers know that you may have to rework the specifications a few times before the project is accepted or dropped. Indeed, you may ask for several first requests at the same time so that you can evaluate the effect of varying aspects of the specification. However, just because it is often necessary to prepare several first estimates does not mean you should ever request information without careful preparation and consultation; that wastes everybody's time.

Final estimates, which are based on the competitive bids from the chosen suppliers, are usually prepared some time after the book is contracted, and often only after the manuscript and other materials have been received, particularly if there is a long gap between the two dates. These estimates are the production department's budget and, barring *unforeseeable* price increases in materials, can be maintained unless there are changes to the criteria on which they are based. Whichever kind of editor you are, you are responsible for those criteria at some point during the gestation of the book. The final estimates, therefore, are as reliable as you are.

Maintaining budgets

Consult before you change

As commissioning editor, you must inform production controllers immediately of any changes to specifications or print runs that occur in the development stages so that they can revise the estimate. The new costs might not affect the viability of the project or they might make you realize that those planned alterations are not such a good idea after all. The same is true if modifications to the specification or schedule (see below) are considered during the copy-editing phase.

Consider the effect of changes even when they are not of your choosing. For example, let us say that the estimates have been prepared on the understanding that the text will be generated from the author's disk with the typesetter inputting editorial alterations. You would need to inform production if the author's disk were unusable for any reason. Having to keyboard the manuscript will affect costs and the schedule. There would be even greater cost and schedule increases if the assumption had been that the entire typesetting and page make-up would be done in-house. Of course, if you are maintaining contact with the author during the writing phase and getting a sample of the text and the disk, you might be able to minimize or preclude such problems (see 'Disks', below).

Weigh the options very carefully when the choice is yours. It is not unknown, for example, for authors to submit texts over the contractual length or include diagrams and tables that had not been agreed, or request more illustrations than planned. Before you agree to any of these or similar alterations, discuss them with production. Do not ask 'Can it be done?' Of course it can. The question for production is 'What will it cost in time and money?' and the question you must then ask and answer yourself is 'How will that affect the profit margin?' If the extra length is really important, discuss with production if there is any way of offsetting the increase in the amount of paper by a saving, say, on the type of paper. If you have a very tight schedule, the answer might be that the paper has already been purchased and not only can you not have another kind, but there is not enough of the one in stock for the increased extent. Perhaps the production controller has another idea. Or perhaps the designer will be able to revise the typography: a more condensed face, a smaller size, less leading, smaller margins, smaller illustrations. Will this new look save the extent? Will it still have the right appearance for the targeted market at the proposed price? Now ask yourself if those extra words are vital. And if they are, review your commissioning process to see how to be more accurate in estimating the appropriate length of text next time.

Did someone suggest that larger illustrations and more colour would increase sales? That might look nice, but discuss the costs with the picture researcher and production, and the sales potential with the sales department. Will the increase in sales balance the increase in costs, or does the original specification now look just right?

A little arithmetic

Think carefully about proof corrections. You know that production controllers always include an amount, calculated as a percentage of the typesetting costs, for author and editor alterations to proofs. Look at it. Do you understand how many corrections that sum allows? A percentage of the cost of typesetting does not equate to correcting that percentage of the text because making corrections takes proportionally more time, and therefore costs more, than continuous keyboarding.

Production controllers can tell you what the typesetting cost is per page for a given book, which will vary according to the number of words and complexity of the setting. They can also tell you what the cost of making a correction is, which will be the same whether the page has many or few words, and is simple or complex. If logic is your strong point, you will quickly realize that the higher the page price, the more corrections can be made within the budget.

To work out the precise number of corrections is simple. Let us say that the price for a page of straight setting is x and the cost of making a correction is y. Dividing y by x translates the cost of a correction into a percentage of the typesetting price. Substitute some numbers to see how easily it works. Say that $x = 2$ and $y = 0.40$. Therefore y is 20% of x. Now, if the correction budget is 10% of the original typesetting cost, that means that the house (author and editor) can make only one correction every two pages. On the other hand, for setting wordier, more complicated pages, x might be 4. As y is still 0.40 (10% of the page cost) you can make one change on every page. Perhaps you are going to supply the text on disk to the typesetter. This will reduce the typesetting costs — let us say x will be 1 — but y is still unchanged at 0.40, or 40% of the page price, so there can be only one correction every four pages.

So far we have considered only straight typesetting corrections. To be in a position to maintain the budget, you need to know more. Talk to your production controller to find out:

- exactly how much more expensive it is when one correction leads to another, such as repagination,
- the increase in cost for making typesetting and layout changes at progressively later stages (page, CRC or film),
- the cost of remaking the film separations for an illustration.

Now you can see that there are several ways for you to keep the cost of corrections within budget.

- When you are discussing the contract with authors, make sure they understand that only serious errors can be corrected at proof stage; it is not an opportunity for rewriting. Use figures to explain the costs for which they could be liable and how delays resulting from heavy or late corrections could affect sales of their book.
- Do not pass materials into production until they are complete, all problems are resolved and the editorial work has been done to the required standard.
- Brief the proofreader about the acceptable level of house alterations to proofs.
- In collating proofs, consider carefully which of the changes that authors have marked are essential, which are desirable and which are unnecessary.
- Apply these same distinctions to changes to text or illustration at any stage of proof. Remember that essential changes are those that will affect the book's sales or the author's or publisher's reputation, or remove a danger to the reader or an element that would contravene a law. All other changes are a matter of choice.
- Do not be deluded that there are no costs when changes are made in-house (see 'Disks', below).
- Do not read Ozalids/blueprints. They are to be checked only for completeness and position.
- Request a higher level of corrections at first estimates for books that are likely to require them, such as those on law or highly topical issues, or those that are being produced on a rush schedule.

Maintaining schedules

We have talked about analysing and maintaining schedules in every chapter. Remember, when production departments draw up schedules, they start from the required publication date and work back through the manufacturing stages to the manuscript delivery date. They establish the critical path — the events shaded in Figure 8.1. They usually have a scale of times to allow for editing and design, and they cannot know whether or not they have picked the right end of the scale or whether the scale applies in each case unless you tell them. If you are initiating the schedule, you have to know how long each manufacturing stage will take.

Discussing editorial, design and production time requirements together before the schedule is planned not only means a timetable to which everyone agrees, but also can influence production's choice of suppliers and raise budget and quality issues. For example, if manufacturing time is curtailed because more time will be needed prepress, production might be able to ensure the publication date by choosing a printer who is faster or nearer but may be more expensive or not of the same quality. With the options made clear at this early stage, you can re-examine your priorities, discuss working practices again with editorial and design colleagues and decide whether the quality desired can be achieved, after all, within the original schedule and budget or where compromises have to be made.

Obviously, after the schedule has been agreed, delays at any stage threaten the publication date or allow it only at increased expense. Being a week late with materials for any outside supplier does not necessarily mean a delay of only a week. Your job has lost its place and will have to wait until it can be fitted in without affecting other jobs. Of course, if you warn production controllers at the very first sign of delay, they might be able to negotiate a new date that ensures the work still gets done on time. Like all of us, they can deal more effectively with a problem than with a crisis, but they cannot always overcome the difficulty completely. Even if they can save time by sending materials by courier or changing printers or revising the means of transporting copies, for example, such action can blow the budget. Remember, too, that the more often you allow scheduling problems to occur, particularly if they reach a critical point, the less often production controllers may be able to help, because your lack of reliability can affect their bargaining power with suppliers. Do not be cavalier. Your first responsibility is to maintain your part of the schedule. If your projects frequently run late, discuss with your colleagues where and why the delays occur, and work out realistic solutions together.

Disks

The decision on which production route to follow — traditional typesetting and composition, disk to typesetter or DTP — should be made before the proposal is accepted on the basis of first estimates, and has to be confirmed before final estimates. Authors have to be briefed on how to prepare disks so that they can be used cost-effectively, and you should get sample disks from new authors well before the delivery date so that you, design and production can check them. Remember, if a text is going to be heavily edited, it is less expensive to have it rekeyed than to make extensive changes to disks. Production will need to verify compatibility of hardware and software with the typesetting system that will be used, and will want confirmation that the typesetter is or is not inputting editorial changes and typographical codes. If the disks do not meet the requirements of any department, you may be able to rebrief authors, editors or designers, or you may have to revise the route the book will take — and revise the schedule and budget as a result.

There is a slight chance that you are thinking that you do not have to worry about the quality of the disks or, indeed, the changes at proof because there are no direct costs for in-house DTP on the estimate request form or the proposal. Think again: there still is a cost. Even if cleaning up the disk is done in-house, someone has to do it, and that someone's time is budgeted. It also costs money to use the machinery. If these activities have not been planned, they have not been budgeted. The money spent might be allocated to overheads rather than to the book, but it is still money.

If you input your editorial changes yourself and produce a printout before typesetting, do not be tempted to re-edit and produce new printouts every time you notice an error. Edit the manuscript as if it were going to an external typesetter, and regard a printout as a proof. Your time and this work has also been budgeted in the overheads; if you take longer, you exceed the budget; if you revise work instead of doing it right the first time, you exceed the budget; if you make two printouts instead of one, you exceed the budget.

Sending and receiving materials

Chapter 6 sets out the basic rules for handing over manuscripts, illustrations and disks (see page 95), which should also be adhered to when working with production. In addition, when you are returning proofs of text or illustrations, check that they are complete, clearly and properly marked, contain no unresolved queries, and are accompanied by any other materials required. Itemize what is in the package and confirm the next scheduled date in a memo or use a proof-return form (see Figure 8.4). It may not always be possible to hand over materials personally. If you leave them on a production controller's desk, send them through the internal mail or ask someone else to hand them over, check later with the production controller that everything, including the schedule, is OK.

Whenever you receive materials from production, check promptly that what you have matches the accompanying memo or delivery note and is what you are expecting. The sooner you notify production that something is missing, the easier it is for them to trace it and the more likely it is to be found.

Date _____

To _____   From _____

Title _____
Author(s)/Editor _____
ISBN _____

Herewith returned:
marked galleys ☐   original hard copy ☐   disks ☐ No. _____
revised proofs ☐   pages ☐   scatterproofs ☐
CRC ☐   Ozalid/blues ☐   other _____

plus
new copy: pp_____–_____
specify No.: _____ pp layouts   _____ transparencies
     _____ halftones   _____ pieces line a/w   _____ tone a/w

For return to me as _____ **on** _____

Figure 8.4 A proof-return form

9

Working with freelancers

Once upon a time the great majority of editors, designers, production controllers, rights and publicity personnel worked in-house and the freelancer was a relative rarity in publishing, most often encountered as picture researchers, indexers and illustrators. Hierarchies, loyalties and relationships between departments were clearly and firmly established, and the lines of communication were identified, if not always working. The great growth in freelance work was initiated by poor economic circumstances and has been facilitated by the advances in computer and telecommunications technology. Now there are freelancers in all the publishing disciplines, and the nature of their work and their ability to do it need not be limited by their proximity to the company offices. Whatever the specific job, all freelancers are suppliers, publishing houses are the clients, and the basic relationship is contractual. For that relationship to be effective, it is essential, as always, to understand your respective roles and responsibilities, and to be proficient communicators.

What's the point?

Companies use freelancers for three main reasons:

- to save time,
- to save money,
- for specialist skills or knowledge.

The savings in time can be viewed in two ways. First, publishers use freelancers to increase the number of titles they could otherwise produce in a given period with only their in-house staff. While individual editors might be able to do all the editorial and liaison work on just a small number of projects at one time, they can increase the number of titles they handle by freelancing time-consuming aspects of the jobs, and multiply their productivity by freelancing whole projects. There is, of course, always some time involved in using freelancers, so the savings for the company are never 100%. Secondly, freelancers are often able to finish a job in a shorter period than in-house staff because they have more control of both their working environment, so they can more easily arrange not to be interrupted or distracted; and their schedule, by deciding how much work to accept, and when and how many hours to work. It should not be assumed from this that all freelancers work more hours a day or more days a week or more weeks in the year than people in-house. Some do, but many work the same amount of time, and others choose to work less.

The financial savings to a publisher are obvious. If you do not work in-house, companies pay only for the work you do and only when they need you to do it. They do not have to pay for space to accommodate you or for any of the utilities you use. They do not have to provide you with the furniture, equipment, books, journals and other supplies that you need. They do not have to calculate, withhold and submit your taxes to government, contribute to your pension scheme, or pay you when you are ill, on maternity or paternity leave, having time off on public holidays or personal vacations, or reading your mail. They do not have to train you or employ assistants for you. Thus they can reduce their capital costs, maintenance and other overheads, and should be able to control their project budgets more tightly (see 'Budgets', below).

A specialist skill is one that you do not have in-house, whether it is as general as proofreading or as unique as illustrating a story. Specialist knowledge may be in a subject area or in preparing texts for particular markets.

Relative savings

Chapter 4 describes different styles of management (see pages 43–4, 57–8), which are the same whether you are are delegating work to someone in-house or to a freelancer: you have to choose the appropriate people for the job, brief them, check the work and provide feedback. The more closely involved you are, the less time you save, but the tighter your control on budgets, schedules and quality. You should be able to maintain control of these factors even when you reduce your involvement to a minimum and maximize the savings in time and overheads. Your choice of style when using a freelancer may depend on the nature of the job, the priorities of speed, cost and quality, or even the individuals you want to use. Whichever style you employ, it is important that you always clearly define roles for yourself and all others involved.

Sources

Personal contacts

Freelancers often write to publishing houses looking for work, and most companies keep these letters on file. Letters that are several years old from individuals whose services have never been tried should be read with the understanding that the skills and experience offered may be different now.

Many people joining a company use the freelancers who work for their colleagues. The advantages are clear: the freelancers have been tried and their work found acceptable, and they have some knowledge of the house style and system. Depending on how well your colleagues check the work they receive and keep records on individual performance, you may be able to use their sources with confidence or you can at least contact the individuals and form your own opinion.

In a company that has not yet established a file of freelancers, you can ask your colleagues if they know people who do freelance work, or advertise internally in a large organization. People in your company might have friends or relatives who work freelance, or they might do so themselves in their own time. While you might be grateful for the contacts, be aware that giving negative feedback might be difficult or embarrassing, and can interfere with your working relationships in-house.

Former staff members often offer their services as freelancers when they leave a company. They know the house style, systems and, of course, other members of the team, and may have built up relationships with some of the authors. The quality of their work is known too. All this can be very useful, particularly if you are new to the company, but it is no excuse for not providing a thorough brief, checking that the work is to the standard you require, and giving feedback. Similarly, when peers or superiors — even bosses — go freelance, keep the freelance relationship professional: you are the client, they are the suppliers.

In publishing, as in any community, there are ways and means to get to know your neighbours if you use your initiative. Contacts in other houses may be able to give you names of freelancers and recommendations. They know that freelancers do not work for them exclusively and may realize that freelancers appreciate being recommended to other firms. Just as you might like this help from others, you should not begrudge such information when you are asked for it.

You can ask freelancers who have to turn down the offer of a job from you if they can suggest or recommend someone else. Make sure you know whether you are simply getting the name of a person to contact or a recommendation based on knowledge of that person's work.

Organizations

Look in the telephone directory and trade journals and on the Internet for societies and associations of freelance workers, particularly editors, proofreaders, indexers and picture researchers. One of the first things such organizations do when they set up is to produce a directory of their members' services. Some societies award their members status based on tests of their competence.

Perhaps there is no appropriate society or no members listed with the special skills you need. Think. Contact colleges, universities and training organizations that offer courses in publishing or in the specialist area in which you need help, or professional institutes and associations; people working there might also freelance or be able to give you the names of others to contact.

Advertisements

Individuals and organizations might advertise their services in trade journals or newspapers. You might find it helpful to advertise in these places and in the newsletters of freelancers' organizations. Think carefully about whom you want to attract — what skills and experience they must have and which are a bonus — and for what purpose. For example, you may be looking for people

- to add to your pool of freelancers,
- for a specific short-term job or long-term project,
- to work in-house or externally,
- to work individually or as part of a team.

First impressions

The view from in-house

In order to feel confident about entrusting work to freelancers, you need to form an opinion about what they can do and in what ways you might use them. Obviously, well-kept freelance files and recommendations from colleagues in-house provide a good foundation. On the other hand, all you may have are a stack of letters, entries in a directory or a list of names and telephone numbers. How you follow up these leads is important. At the beginning of what might be new working relationships, freelancers will be forming opinions about you and even about the house for which you work.

Look at the letters. Presentation is an important part of all publishing tasks and letters are a reflection of the quality of work that people produce. Therefore, if the information in a letter is poorly organized or badly expressed, or the layout and typing are inferior, do not waste your time investigating its author further.

Next, examine the information. You are trying to find freelancers with relevant skills, in relevant subjects and, ideally, with relevant in-house experience if they are editors or proofreaders. Obviously, therefore, you will reject offers from people who work exclusively in subject areas not on your list. In-house experience indicates not only that individuals have worked but also that they have some knowledge of all the activities and relationships, and probably some of the problems, involved in producing books, journals and other publications, which can make them better equipped to work effectively in their relative isolation; this point is not relevant to picture researchers or indexers. You might decide not to pursue people who have little or no experience of any kind because you do not have the time to train them; remember, one of the main reasons for using freelancers is to save time. Or you might realize that there is an insufficient number of fully trained freelancers in your locale or subject area, or with the specific skills, particularly computer skills, that you need. Then you might decide that it is a good investment to spend the time training people to provide yourself with freelancers moulded to your requirements.

Contact people who seem promising and from whom you want more information. Ask them, for example, for any of the following information that you need and is not either stated or implicit in their letter or directory entry.

- Where did they get their training? It might have been on courses or it might have been in-house.
- What areas do they specialize in and are there any that they choose not to work in?
- For whom have they freelanced in the past? Their letter or entry probably lists the publishing houses, but ask for the names of individuals who can act as referees. Contact at least some of these people to find out about a potential freelancer's speed, reliability, range of experience, quality of work, and communication skills. Make your questions as precise as possible and relevant to the work you might want the individual to undertake so that you get useful information.
- What types of publication do they work on? Perhaps you need someone experienced in working on loose-leafs, encyclopedias, directories or spread-by-spread books.
- Do they work full-time, and, if not, how many hours a week generally? Freelancers may have commitments to other houses for one or two days a week, or they might want to work only part-time. You need to know that when considering the schedule for the job you want done.
- Do they work on-screen and, if so, what hardware and software do they have?
- What is their usual rate? Most rates are negotiable and your company may have a house rate, but you need to know if the two are within reasonable range of each other.

As well as, or before, talking to potential editors and proofreaders, especially those who cannot supply references, you might ask them to complete a test. Alternatively, you might try them out on a simple job, which is also an appropriate way to test indexers and picture researchers. If you are commissioning illustrators and photographers directly, rather than through a designer, you should, of course, ask to see their portfolio.

The view from outside

Freelancers will not be able to form any opinion of you if they have addressed their letter to a job title, such as managing editor or editorial director, or to the human resources department, and receive no reply. However, they will still judge your company: is it so poorly organized or does it care so little for people that it cannot manage to acknowledge their communication, and how might that be reflected in the way it treats the freelancers it does use? Word gets around, and you may find that your firm is not one that freelancers are eager to work for.

It is so easy to avoid creating a bad impression: acknowledge every letter you receive from a freelancer. Sending a *pertinent* written reply — a letter or even a postcard — when you do not wish to offer work at the moment or at all is not a time-consuming task and you can streamline it by preparing a number of standard responses. For example:

- the experience or skills offered are not relevant to your area of publishing,
- the applicant does not have sufficient experience or the appropriate skills,
- the skills and experience are suitable, but you do not have any work to offer right now and will keep the letter on file.

More teamwork

If you have a sufficient flow of work, build up a band of reliable freelancers — individuals whose services you use regularly, although not constantly or exclusively, throughout the year. Develop a second corps of freelancers to use when the regulars are busy and sometimes even when they are not, to keep the 'understudies' interested in working for you and in touch with your house style and requirements. Teams are built up and renewed over time. Bring in new people as required to give you access to new skills and to replace those who leave.

Keep clear, concise and well-organized records (see Figure 9.1) so that you can easily select an appropriate person for each job (see Chapter 4, pages 51–2) and spread the work around the team, which can help prevent individuals from getting into a rut. Note the titles worked on, keep comments brief and objective, and date remarks. If the records are kept centrally so that they are available to other people in-house, everyone should also sign or initial their entries so that colleagues know from whom they might get more information.

As you become aware of people's strengths and weaknesses, you will be able to target work more accurately, and determine who is in the first rank and who in the second. There might be some freelancers who have been recommended or seem very experienced but who do not produce the kind or quality of work you need and do

Date:	8/8/97
Name:	A Freelancer
Postal address:	121 First Street, Little Town
e-mail address:	afreelancer@central.com.co
Telephone:	111-1111
Fax:	111-2222
Services offered:	copy-editing, rewriting; works on-screen on Mac in Word and Quark
General subjects:	arts and humanities
Specialist subjects:	twentieth-century history, modern art
Exclusions:	war, militaria, religious doctrine, gardening
Types of book:	illustrated, co-editions, all levels
Availability:	full-time, not in-house
Notes:	*Art in Our Time*: good visualizer; handled complex job well, weak on foreign language spelling, accents. 11/11/97; *A Day on the Train*: good co-edition job, kept tight schedules. 4/4/98; *Psych Talk*: heavy rewrite, author very pleased 7/7/98.

Figure 9.1 A freelancer's record

not respond positively to the feedback you give them (see below). Even if they produce work that satisfies your colleagues, there is no place for them on either of your
teams. It is also important to keep an eye on the freelancers you use regularly, so you
can give them a rest or change of pace if their work starts to slip in quality (see also
'Feedback', below).

Scheduling

Good freelancers are busy. If you want to use their services, you need to approach
them in advance, and you need to give yourself enough time to find or select and
approach others if the first person you try turns down the job. Depending on the
number of freelancers available and the amount of work they can get from any
source, this might mean six to eight weeks, and more for some specialists. Your
global schedule (see Chapter 4, page 50) should indicate when the manuscript is
due in-house and the dates when you will need freelancers for particular tasks.
Remember, schedules for all freelance work need to take into account the time
taken for the job to travel between you and the freelancer.

Stages of engagement

Approaching copy-editors before you have the manuscript in-house might seem a problem: how can you give them a brief or even a reliable schedule if you do not have the materials? However, when you look at it in detail, the problem dissolves. First, ask yourself what you need to know at this point. The answer seems clear: you need to find out only whether freelancers are:

- interested in working on this subject and, if new to you, for your company,
- experienced in the type of work and subject area,
- available when you need them,
- affordable.

In order to answer your questions, freelancers have to consider:

- the subject of the project,
- the number of words,
- how complex the job is; for example, will the manuscript involve tables, references or artwork,
- the proposed level of involvement; that is, whether they will be working with the author and other team members, and to what stage of production,
- the date the work will be sent,
- how many hours or days it is likely to take,
- the date it must be returned,
- the fee or hourly rate.

Even if you have not seen any sample materials, you can find out the subject, extent and complexity by reading the proposal. Examining your global schedule and the budget will help you decide what style of management to use, which indicates the freelancers' level of involvement as well as your own. A publication date has also been proposed, so you can work out, with design and production, when the materials have to be sent out and returned; even when these dates change, as they often do, planning now gives you a useful framework. When the project is similar to others or you have seen sample material, it is easier to estimate roughly how long the job will take. Freelancers, like their in-house counterparts, work on a number of titles simultaneously and will have to assess whether they will have enough time within the scheduled period to do your job. Make sure that the schedule also allows time for the materials to be in transit; for freelancers to assimilate the brief and, if they are new to your firm, the house style, to complete handover forms and deal with queries; and for you to check the completed work.

After freelancers have agreed to take a job, confirm the arrangements in writing. Your job now is to maintain the schedule, which also means coping with any interruptions. Everyone in publishing knows that delays can occur, and they do not damage your standing with freelancers as long as you are seen to be in control generally and provide adequate warning. If you are maintaining contact with the author prior to manuscript delivery date, you should have a good idea whether the project will start on time. After it begins, you need to ensure that each freelancer sticks to the schedule or informs you of delays (see 'Briefs', below) so that you can inform other in-house and freelance team members of the disruption. Even if the delay is only a few days or a week, freelancers might have to rearrange their own work to accommodate it. If the work will be held up for longer, freelancers might have to renegotiate the schedule with you or turn down the job because of other commitments. Until you have established a reputation for reliability with freelancers, you might want to telephone them a week before you are supposed to send materials to assure them the date will be kept.

When the project materials arrive in-house and you assess them (see Chapter 4), you will be able to check the accuracy of the schedule, revise it if necessary and inform freelancers of changes affecting them. Monitoring the accuracy of your estimates can help you to improve them. For example, if there is frequently a disparity between your evaluation of the time needed before and after you see the materials, you might be able to distinguish which aspects of the job you are neglecting to take into account or to which you are not allocating enough time initially. Notice too if freelancers are consistently taking more time than planned to complete tasks and plan future schedules with this longer time in mind. When jobs always come in on time, you can ask a few of the freelancers on your first team whether shorter schedules would be adequate.

Briefs

Earlier chapters have dealt with assessing the project and preparing the brief for copy-editors and proofreaders (Chapter 4), indexers (Chapter 5), designers (Chapter 6) and picture researchers (Chapter 7). When those individuals are freelance, the briefs must be written and include payment details. You can streamline this procedure by using a handover form (see Figure 3.1, on pages 40–1) to list all the items being sent and a checklist for the tasks to be done (Figure 9.2). Your covering letter can then focus on information about the market, the series and the author; main problems with the manuscript or associated materials; and exceptions to the house style or other usual requirements, particularly those previously agreed with the author. It should always ask freelancers to confirm the schedule and the fee, and invite them to contact you if they want to discuss the work or foresee a delay.

Copy-edit

On hard copy ❏
  key in tables & illustrations ❏
  separate tables, figures from text ❏

On disk
  input editorial changes ❏
  tag and code for setting ❏
  check file management ❏
  place tables, figs, captions,
    notes in separate files ❏
  format output as _____
  cut and fill pages as required ❏

Level of edit
  minimal ❏
  medial ❏
  major ❏

Cut/expand by _____ %/words

Check/clear permissions ❏
Check acknowledgements ❏

Queries
  resolve with author ❏
  send to project editor ❏

Prepare briefs for
  artwork ❏
  photography ❏
  picture research ❏
  index ❏

Liaise with
  designer ❏
  illustrator ❏
  picture researcher ❏
  indexer ❏
  production ❏

Proofread

Galleys
  against copy ❏
  blind ❏
  include separate list of
    queries ❏
  highlight x-refs to folios ❏
  key in tables & illustrations ❏

Pages
  against galleys ❏
  check optimum position of
    tables & illustrations ❏
  fill in x-ref folios ❏
  fill in folios on Contents ❏
  check running heads ❏

Index
  galleys ❏
  pages ❏

Collate

Proofreaders' & authors' galleys ❏

Figure 9.2 A checklist of tasks

A few days after you send a project, phone the freelancer to discuss it. Check that the brief has been clearly understood and that the freelancer has all the materials, has had an opportunity to look through the job, and can confirm the schedule and the fee.

Checking projects

Checking individual stages of work has been covered in previous chapters, but when you are dealing with freelancers, you may also want to check how the work is progressing if they have a long schedule. Telephone at intervals to find out how they are getting on; it may provide them with an opportunity to discuss problems that have arisen or decisions they have taken, and for you to retain a peripheral involvement in the project.

To control quality, schedule and budgets when you reduce your involvement to a minimum by freelancing an entire project from manuscript to CRC, supervise jobs by arranging for freelance project managers to report to you and submit materials at key stages. Thus you would expect to see and have time to spot check:

- specimen pages
- illustrations
- galleys/printout
- page proofs
- cover/jacket design and blurb

You can, and should, still retain contact with authors, so that they always have the continuity and security of dealing with someone in-house.

Budgets

The budgets for freelance work should be included as direct costs in the publishing proposal (see Chapter 2, page 26). The costs for individual tasks are based on an hourly rate. Even when quoted as a fee or a per-page rate, they are calculated on an estimate of the amount of time the job will take — including time spent going to the nearest post office and waiting to send a package — plus reimbursement for expenses and a small amount for contingencies. The costs for project managers have to include the amounts for each of the separate tasks for which they are responsible, which may include manufacturing costs to CRC, plus a management fee.

Although it may not be common, projects can be cancelled. Obviously, you should give freelancers as much notice as possible if this happens before they begin work. However, if notice is less than a week or the project is cancelled after freelancers have begun work, you should negotiate reasonable compensation, for they will have turned down other work for the period of time that your job would have occupied.

Rates of pay

Your firm may have a range of rates that it is willing to pay for different tasks. This makes it is easier to control the relationship between the nature of the work needed and the price at which the book will be sold; the more complex, technical or specialized the job, the higher the rate and usually the higher the price of the book. Thus it is appropriate to pay more for proofreading against copy than for proofreading 'blind'; more for copy-editing than for proofreading, and more for copy-editing academic texts than for copy-editing non-specialist books. Work done on computer should attract higher rates than that done only on paper because it requires more skills as well as special equipment.

In addition to the nature of the task, you should also expect and be willing to pay more for higher quality and greater experience. The quality of the work can affect the sales potential of books and the reputations of the authors and the company; the freelancers' experience can save time and money because it enables them to foresee and cope with a wider range of problems that might arise. You may also have to pay more for jobs completed on a rush, as opposed to a merely tight, schedule, because of the extra effort, and probably unsocial hours, required.

Freelancers may have a range of rates they are willing to accept. They are operating a business and, like any business, their rates reflect the nature of the work they do, their experience and their overheads; all the savings the company makes by not having people in-house (see page 130) are the overheads that freelancers have to support. Individuals may offer a number of services, some of which pay better than others. Overall, they try to achieve a balance of regular work, satisfaction and a reasonable income. However, even if the category of work is lower paying — proofreading rather than copy-editing, a superficial rather than in-depth edit — you will pay at the higher end of the range for an experienced freelancer of high quality.

Market forces play a role for both publishers and freelancers. Publishers are competing for the services of the freelancers, and freelancers are competing with each other for the work. If you want to secure the services of any freelancers, you have to know what the current market rates are — what freelancers charge and what other firms pay (associations of freelancers will be able to tell you) — and if you plan to use good freelancers, your rates must be competitive. Be prepared to negotiate, to find a compromise between what you offered initially and what they aim to get. Freelancers who are in demand can pick which jobs to accept (see 'Maintaining good relations', below). Put yourself in their position: would you choose to work for a company that pays poorly? The simple answer is that low pay does not attract high-quality work.

Some publishers offer freelancers a fee because they see this as a way to avoid comparisons with other firms' hourly rates and to control the budget absolutely.

However, this is the same as proposing an hourly rate for a maximum number of hours, and freelancers will simply divide a fee by the number of hours the job is estimated to take to see what the rate equivalent is.

Expenses

Freelancers are reimbursed for expenses incurred in doing the job. Therefore you will pay for:

- their telephone calls, faxes and e-mail to anyone other than yourself, such as authors, consultants, libraries, picture agencies, other information sources and other team members with whom you have asked them to liaise,
- postage and courier charges,
- fares at the lowest reasonable rate — buses rather than taxis, for example — for journeys *necessitated* by the work.

You should state the maximum amount of expenses whenever it is likely to be substantial, as is more often the case for picture researchers and project managers than proofreaders or copy-editors. Very small expenses can be met by the contingency part of the budget. You can reduce expenses and the direct costs on the project by letting picture researchers send all their mail through the company; either way the company pays, but overheads spread the costs among all the books rather than directing them at one.

Contingency

This is a relatively small amount of the total freelance budget on the project that you hold aside to pay for extra costs that might be incurred. Even after you and the freelancers have confirmed the fee for a job, they might encounter a problem while working that was not expected and could not be foreseen. Always make it clear to freelancers in your briefing letter that they should contact you as soon as this situation arises to discuss how much extra time and money will be involved so that you can check the budget and schedule and decide what to do.

Payment

You want the work done on schedule and freelancers want to be paid on time. It's a fair deal. Most companies operate a monthly accounting system. Tell your freelancers when the month-end is, so that if they miss the closing date for invoices in one month, they will be able to calculate the number of weeks before their invoice will be paid. If they are on a long job, agree a schedule of interim payments.

You do not control the company's cashflow, but you have to be aware that freelancers cannot afford to work for companies that do not pay promptly. Freelancers do not enjoy having to chase companies for money owed, and they should not have to do it. Their communication network may be stronger than that in your firm, and they will know if your company gains a reputation for payment delays and prevarication. They can choose not to work for you.

Feedback

Feedback can help freelancers to improve generally and to become more aware of your firm's particular requirements, and it is important to developing a good working relationship. As Chapter 4 explains, feedback that is given soon after the job is done, and is specific, constructive and objective is most likely to have the desired effect.

The difference between giving feedback to an in-house colleague and a freelancer is in how you deliver it. You can talk to your in-house colleagues face to face, but you usually have to deal with freelancers at a distance. Occasionally, a postcard or short, informal letter is sufficient when you simply want to acknowledge receipt of people's work and thank them for a job well done, although a telephone call is more useful for developing a relationship. This kind of personal contact is also more important when you want to point out problems that arose or improvements that are needed. You can discuss relatively minor issues and judge from the other person's tone of voice how the information is being received. Major or numerous problems might be difficult to absorb over the phone, and freelancers might become defensive. However, it is useful to telephone to introduce the subject and prepare the freelancers for the letter in which you explain the detail, indicating in that letter that they can call you if, after considering the issues, they want to discuss them. This gives them time to come to terms with the criticism and realize that you have also made positive comments.

Some freelancers might be older and more experienced than you are. Maintaining a friendly, professional approach and being willing to learn from them does not mean being subservient, just open-minded. If they refute your criticism, consider what they have to say. Give yourself space to change your mind. If you are sure of your ground, try to explain the point more clearly and give the freelancers the opportunity to change their mind too.

Reminding people on subsequent jobs of points raised in feedback is useful reinforcement. There might be lengthy intervals between the two jobs, during which they will be working for other companies that might have very different requirements. Putting such comments in the brief also reminds you to check those points and to monitor the strengths and weaknesses of your freelancers.

Maintaining good relations

Your aim is to build a relationship with people you might never see. Good communications with people out of house is essential; they will respond to you on the basis of how you approach and treat them. Freelancers value a professional approach. This means that you:

- contact them a reasonable amount of time before you need their services,
- provide a clear brief,
- are reliable, sending what you promise when you promise it, and warning of changes to the schedule or other aspects of the job,
- offer reasonable rates,
- pay promptly,
- provide a free copy of the book if wanted,
- provide feedback.

In addition, you might offer staff discounts for books, put freelancers on your catalogue mailing list and send them the company newsletter, or arrange an annual freelance social event.

Good relationships reap rewards. If you treat freelancers well in all these ways, make them feel valued, and offer interesting work at reasonable intervals, they might choose to work for you even if your rates of pay are not the highest. They might also be willing occasionally to do you a favour, like squeezing a last-minute rush job into their otherwise full schedule. And the relationship will transfer with you if you move to another publisher.

10

Copyright and permissions

Copyright exists in specified types of work and protects them from being copied without the permission of their owners except in certain circumstances. Such a good, simple idea. However, for rights to be protected, there must be laws that define them and the conditions of protection. While many countries agree with this principle, their laws vary in detail. New laws can alter conditions substantially, but they are not retroactive, so it may be necessary to know the terms of more than one Act in any country (see also 'Ownership and rights', below). For example, in the United Kingdom the Copyright, Designs and Patents Act 1988 came into force on 1 August 1989, replacing the Copyright Act 1956, and was amended in January 1996 on the implementation of a European Directive. In the United States the current law, the Copyright Act of 1976, took effect on 1 January 1978, superseding previous federal law and common law, and was amended on 31 October 1988 to bring its terms into line with the requirements of the Berne Convention (see 'Copyright conventions', below). In both countries the changes in law affected the ownership and duration of copyright (see Figure 10.1), and you may need to find out not only when a work was created but also when and where it was published and who owns the copyright to know which laws apply to it.

These are the reasons why copyright law is so complex. Complex does not mean incomprehensible, of course, and it is your responsibility to understand the law or laws relevant to the books and materials with which you are involved. This chapter discusses the main principles of copyright relating to literary, dramatic and artistic works. You will need to consult books on copyright and media law for explanations and interpretations of the details and for information about other areas of copyright, such as music, sound recording and broadcasting.

Existence versus protection

Copyright exists as soon as an original work in one of the specified categories is created in a material form whether or not that work is ever published. 'Original' refers to the way in which an idea is expressed; it does not have to be unique, but it must

United Kingdom

The duration of copyright as established by the Copyright, Designs and Patents Act 1988 and amended by European Directive 93/98 on 1 July 1995 applies to works still in copyright on 31 December 1995 and works published thereafter.

- *Single author:* The life of the author plus 70 years from the end of the calendar year in which the author dies.

- *Joint authors:* The life of the authors plus 70 years from the end of the calendar year marking the death of the author who died last.

- *Pseudonymous and anonymous authors:* 70 years from the end of the calendar year in which the work was first made available to the public. If the identity of the author is discoverable by reasonable means within this period, the full term of copyright applies.

- *Works unpublished during the lifetime of the author:* Under the Copyright Act 1956, 50 years from the end of the calendar year in which it was first published or performed in public; under the 1989 Act, 50 years from the end of the calendar year when the author dies; for works by authors who died before 1 August 1989 and whose work was not published or performed in public during their lifetime, 50 years from the end of the calendar year in which the Act came into force — 31 December 2039.

- *Corporate ownership:* 50 years from the end of the calendar year of publication.

Revived copyright
Works that went out of copyright in the United Kingdom under the 50-year rule but were still in copyright in another European Union country on 1 July 1995 had their United Kingdom copyright extended for the remainder of the 70-year period. Copyright was not infringed by publication of a new edition without permission if arrangements for publication were made before 1 January 1995 or copies were printed before 1 July 1995 and published after 1 January 1996.

Figure 10.1 Duration of copyright in literary, dramatic and artistic work

United States

Works published before 1 January 1978

- Copyright for works published before 1 January 1964 had to be renewed or would have expired 28 years after publication; for works published after that date renewal is automatic and lasts for 47 years; for works in their second term of copyright as of 1 January 1978, the duration is automatically extended to 47 years.

Works published on or after 1 January 1978

- *Single author:* The life of the author plus 50 years from the end of the calendar year in which the author dies.

- *Joint authors:* The life of the authors plus 50 years from the end of the calendar year marking the death of the author who died last.

- *Pseudonymous and anonymous authors:* 75 years from the end of the calendar year in which the work was first made available to the public or 100 years from the end of the calendar year of creation, whichever is shorter. If, after publication, the identity of the author is revealed and recorded in the Copyright Office, the regular term of copyright applies.

- *Corporate ownership or works made for hire:* 75 years from the date of publication, or 100 years from the date of creation, whichever is shorter.

Unpublished works

- *Works unpublished during the lifetime of the author before 1 January 1978:* Under state laws, until publication, and under Federal law, for 28 years thereafter, renewable for varying terms depending on the date of renewal. All works published on or after 1 January 1906 were still in copyright on 1 January 1978.

- *Works unpublished before 1 January 1978:* The same terms apply as for works created after that date, with copyright enduring until at least 31 December 2002. If the works are published or performed in public prior to that date, copyright lasts until at least 31 December 2027, and longer if their authors lived beyond the end of 1977.

not be copied from another source. Ideas themselves have no material form — they cannot be seen, heard or touched — and therefore cannot have copyright. Material that is not in copyright — either because it was never eligible or because the copyright has expired — is, by definition, in the public domain, which means that anyone can copy it and use it as they like without permission.

National laws differ on the categories of works to which they extend copyright, but in most countries they include literary, dramatic, musical and artistic works, sound recordings and films. These laws may also differ on what is included in each category; for example, in the United Kingdom the category of musical works includes only the music — words to be sung or spoken with the music are considered literary works — while in the United States the music category includes accompanying words. United Kingdom law also has categories for broadcasts and cable programmes, and for the typographical arrangement of published editions that are not mirrored in all other countries although protection may be given.

Giving notice

Although copyright exists from the moment a work is created, giving notice of ownership of that copyright is the most effective way to protect it. For all forms of written matter, a notice of ownership should be placed on every copy. Even when this is not a requirement of national law, it is recommended because it prevents people who infringe copyright from defending their actions by claiming they did not know that the material was in copyright or from claiming that the copyright is theirs. In some countries the courts will reduce the amount of damages if the plaintiffs did not take this simple step to protect their material.

The copyright notice consists of three parts, although the order of the second two varies from country to country:

1   the symbol ©, required by the Universal Copyright Convention (see 'Copyright Conventions', below), or the word 'Copyright',
2   the year of publication,
3   the name of the copyright owner.

The phrase 'All rights reserved' was adopted to provide some protection in those countries that are not signatories to any of the international agreements. The longer forms, like the one printed in this book, set out clearly and in detail what that means so that there is no excuse for infringement.

The copyright notice must be placed in such a way as to give 'reasonable notice' to consumers. Books published in the United Kingdom, North America and Australasia, for example, usually carry the notice on the title verso, while those published in many other countries place it on the last page.

Copyright conventions

There are more than a dozen international agreements to protect some aspect of copyright, of which the two most relevant to publishers are the Berne Convention for the Protection of Literary and Artistic Works, and the Universal Copyright Convention (UCC). They set minimum standards for the terms of national copyright law and require countries to give works by the nationals of other member countries the same protection as they give works by their own nationals. The variation in the duration of copyright in different countries can, for this reason, produce complications when seeking permissions for material to be included in international editions (see 'Permissions', below). For example, if a book originating in the United States, where the duration of copyright is the life of the author plus 50 years, is published in any member state of the European Union, where copyright continues for 70 years from the death of the author, the American work will remain in copyright for that longer period in those countries. However, if the work was made for hire (see 'Ownership and rights', below), copyright will endure for 75 years from the date of publication in the United States, but for only 70 years from the end of the calendar year of publication in the United Kingdom.

Of all the countries that belong to these conventions, more than half are signatories to both, and slightly more than half of the remaining countries are members of Berne.

Ownership and rights

Initially, the person who creates the work owns the copyright unless he or she does so as an employee or makes a work for hire, the conditions governing which vary internationally. For example, in the United States commissioned works in nine limited categories can be works for hire if the creator and the commissioner sign a written agreement to that effect, while in the United Kingdom copyright in all commissioned work belongs to the creator. In both countries these aspects of the current law differ from the terms of preceding law, which still govern many pre-existing works.

The copyright owner of literary and dramatic works has the exclusive right to:

- make copies of the work in any material form, including electronic,
- issue copies of the work to the public,
- perform, display or play the work in public,
- broadcast the work or include it in a cable programme,
- adapt or prepare derivatives of the work.

The copyright owner of artistic works has the same rights except the sole right to display the work.

It is an infringement of copyright to do any of the above without the permission of the copyright owner, except for those incidents that are described as 'fair use' or 'fair dealing' (see 'What's fair?', below). Paraphrasing a substantial amount of copyright material without permission is also an infringement; it is interpreted as disguised copying.

These rights can be sold, assigned, licensed or given away in whole or in part to any person or organization the owner chooses. The author's contract, which underpins the author–publisher relationship, formally acknowledges ownership of the copyright and the terms on which the publisher will pay the writer (the fee or royalty) for permission to exercise the main rights of printing and publishing, and to administer the subsidiary rights, which cover all those areas that the publisher cannot, or chooses not to, exploit itself, such as book club, foreign language and performance rights. Remember, writers are not the only authors, and the rights in the work of artists, photographers, translators and indexers are also subject to contract.

Illustrations

Under current copyright law in both the United States and the United Kingdom, illustrators and photographers are the first owners of the copyright in their work unless they are on the publisher's staff or making a work for hire.

Where artwork illustrates specific points in an author's text, as in diagrams, charts, graphs and simple drawings, it is common for illustrators to part with their copyright for a fee, because they probably will not be able to sell the same pictures to another publisher. There must be a written contract for the transfer of copyright, and the artists are still entitled to be acknowledged as the author of their work (see 'Moral rights', below). However, when the illustrations are as integral to the book as the text, as in children's books, or are complete and comprehensible independent of the text, artists will want to retain their copyright. If you want the *exclusive* rights to reproduce the illustrations, you will need to have a contract stipulating the terms and conditions of use. Think carefully about possible future domestic and foreign editions, use in other books and, for some work, merchandising spin-offs.

Freelance photographers, like illustrators, may be willing to part with the copyright to their images for a fee unless they can exploit the photographs further economically, selling them to other publishers and for other purposes. For example, photographs taken of children doing a science experiment, of a particular chef's recipe or of a completed craft project have no resale value. On the other hand, pictures of general subjects, such as plants, animals and landscapes, can be used repeatedly in different contexts. There must be a written agreement with commissioned photographers for the transfer of copyright or for the *exclusive* licence to reproduce the pictures.

Owning copyright, not the object

Copyright belongs to authors even when they part with the material form of creation. Writers continue to own their copyright when they hand over their manuscripts, and artists and photographers can sell their works and retain their copyrights. If you write letters to your Aunt Maud, she cannot publish them without your permission, because, although she has the letters, you have the copyright.

Moral rights

Moral rights are distinct from copyright even though they may be included in the same law and apply only to works entitled to copyright protection. The laws of all the signatories to the Berne Convention include moral rights, but the details vary from country to country. In the United Kingdom the moral rights are:

1. the right to be identified as the author, which could be called the right of attribution but is nonsensically known as the right of paternity,
2. the right of integrity, which means a work may not be treated in a 'derogatory' way, that is one that would damage the author's reputation,
3. the right not to have a work falsely attributed to you,
4. the right of privacy to photographs and films commissioned for private use.

The 1988 Act defines the circumstances in which these rights apply and any exceptions. Only the first right has to be asserted in writing; the others are inherent if they are applicable. All these rights except the third last for the full term of copyright even if the author ceases to own the copyright; the third subsists for 20 years after the author's death. None of the rights can be assigned, but all can be waived.

In the United States federal Copyright Act, the rights of attribution and integrity apply only to works of fine art of which there are less than 200 copies, although the rights of attribution and against false attribution exist in other federal and state laws.

What's fair?

There are circumstances in which a part of a copyright work can be used without permission. Such practice is called 'fair use' or 'fair dealing'. Some publishers operate on a rule of thumb that up to 400 or 500 words can be reproduced without consent as long as the purpose is criticism or review. It is not that simple.

As always, the detail varies internationally, but there is general agreement that copying for the purposes of research, private study, criticism, review, news reporting, certain educational and library uses constitutes fair dealing. The portion of a work that can be used fairly is *not specified*. It is *interpreted* — which means the judgement is subjective — by its length and importance relative to the whole work and to the work in which it is being reproduced. Thus it would not be safe to quote 400 words without permission if they were:

- extracted from an article only 1000 words long,
- the most vital part, the essence, of an even longer work,
- from a long work but forming the main part, in length or substance, of the work in which they are quoted.

Similarly, in a book it would be fair dealing to quote a stanza from an epic poem but not from one only four stanzas long, and quoting even single lines from a haiku obviously requires consent, which is also strongly advised when quoting lyrics. No copyright material, however short the extract, can be used in an anthology without permission.

The use of illustrations is evaluated in the same way, but the interpretation can be more problematic. For example, in children's books all the illustrations might be seen as a continuous, united whole from which another author might 'quote'. However, each illustration is a complete painting, and reproducing one in another book, even for the purpose of criticism or review, would not be fair dealing, although reproducing it in a book review in a newspaper or magazine might be.

Graphs and charts are also illustrations. They might have been prepared as artwork by the author of the text and be considered individually a small part of the whole work. However, their relative importance to the original source as well as to the publication in which they are to be reprinted must be considered, and may well differ if one source is an article and the other a book, if both are articles, or both are books. The situation will also be different if the artwork was prepared by someone other than the writer, in which case the copyright will be separate from that in the text. In that case it is probable that each chart or graph will be viewed as a complete work and cannot be reused without permission. There is, of course, nothing preventing an author from using the same information to create his or her own *original* charts and graphs.

The restrictions governing fair dealing protect the economic rights of the copyright owner. They can be seen as preventing authors from benefiting more from the quoted work than from their own effort, and even from damaging the quoted work's potential sales.

While fair dealing does not require consent from the copyright owner, it does require sufficient acknowledgement to be made at least to the work and the author, and usually to the publisher as well.

To ask or not to ask

There may be times when you or your authors are uncertain whether fair dealing applies. Review the principles and test your case against them. Consult more experienced colleagues. Then, if you are reasonably sure that the use is fair, do not ask permission; you might pay fees unnecessarily. If, however, you think your case is weak, particularly if you have a nagging suspicion that you or your author is being evasive — perhaps to avoid work or cost, or to preserve a schedule — seek consent; damages for infringement can be embarrassing and expensive.

Permissions

An author must have the copyright owner's permission to use copyright material of any kind, except in instances of fair dealing. If your author's book is going to be published worldwide, remember that material that might be out of copyright in one country could still be in copyright in another. Brief authors to keep clear, comprehensive notes about all the sources from which they quote *as they work*. Consider providing authors, particularly novices and non-academics, with a sheet of paper with the appropriate headings to use as a template (see Figure 10.2). This information is needed for the acknowledgements even if the material can be used without permission, and it is very time-consuming and often impossible for authors to find all the details later. It can be difficult for authors to know at a glance what is in or out of copyright, so it is safest to tell them to record all modern sources, including modern translations or edited editions of work in the public domain. Then you can indicate which quotations need permissions.

Location in ms	Taken from					
	Author	Title and edn	Publisher	Place	Year	pp
p.15	J.S. Simple	Easy Does It	Bookmaker	NY	1981	99
fig. 4	Charles Dots	Diagrams Today, 2nd edn	Tomes	London	1990	122

Figure 10.2 A template for recording sources

Including copyright material in databases, multimedia and other electronic publications may involve more complicated permissions and payment arrangements, but the same principles of copyright law apply. It is in these areas that the law is continuing to evolve most rapidly, so keep up to date with reports in newspapers and trade journals.

Who to ask and how to do it

It is usual to request permissions from the publishers because they often control the subsidiary rights. If they do not, or if they control only some of those you request, they will forward your letter to the appropriate person — the author, an agent, the executor of the literary estate, or another publisher — or tell you to whom to apply. For example, they might be able to grant you rights in the English language in certain countries and give you the name of the publishers who hold those rights for other languages or in other countries. You will have to get permission from the copyright holders in all the territories in which you intend to distribute your book. It is sensible to mention in subsequent requests that you have already obtained permission from the first source.

Some firms require their authors to clear permissions, others do the work but require the authors to pay the fees. Whoever is doing the work, it is helpful and time-saving to have form letters for requesting permissions (see Figure 10.3). Ideally, authors should photocopy the materials they want to reproduce rather than identifying paragraphs, tables or figures by numbers and pages; it prevents those easy-to-make typographical errors leading to confusion and delay at both ends.

You can ask for rights in one or more languages in one or more specific countries, but if the title is likely eventually to be published in more than two or three languages or countries, it is administratively simpler and less expensive to ask for world rights (all languages in all countries). Similarly, if the publication is a book, volume rights for all editions allow you to publish revised editions, book club editions and different bindings without having to reapply, and pay again, for permission. If the the book is likely to be extracted or serialized, it would also be wise to ask for the right to grant permission for the quoted material to be used in that context. Obviously, you must indicate if your title will be published instead or also as a CD-Rom or electronically. Be sure to state if the title is a schoolbook: the fees requested are usually lower.

All permissions should be in writing. Even if the author has done the work, you need the documents so that you can check that all necessary permissions have been obtained, can incorporate the wording required in the acknowledgements (see 'Acknowledgements', below), and, when the company is paying, check that the total costs are within budget.

Date

Dear ...

Reference

We request permission to reproduce the text/figure attached, which appeared in your publication:

Author/editor, Title, date of publication, page(s)

The material is to appear in the following title that we are preparing for publication:

Author/editor, Title
Extent
Planned date of publication
Proposed price and print run
Rights desired (languages/territories/form of publication)

We will, of course, give full acknowledgement to the author, title and publisher, but please inform us if additional information or a particular form of wording is required. Please also let us know if we must seek permission from another source for any or all of the rights requested.

Figure 10.3 Example of a permission form letter from a publishing house. If authors are clearing permissions, they should give the name of their publisher after the title.

Photographs

Publishers of illustrated books usually pay for both the picture research (see Chapter 7) and the fees for the use of photographs. There are two kinds of fee — copyright and reproduction. The people or organizations that own the prints and transparencies do not necessarily own the copyright, which may have expired or be owned by someone else (see 'Owning copyright, not the object', above). In this case, the fee they are charging you is for the right to use their physical property for reproduction. They should tell you if the copyright is owned by someone else who will need to be acknowledged, and whether you have to apply separately for copyright permission or it is included in the current transaction.

Sometimes the same print or transparency is available from another source, and picture researchers will then look for the source to suit your budget, schedule and quality requirements. Although it might be possible to commission a photographer to take a similar picture, it may not be economical to do so.

No permission is needed for the incidental inclusion of a copyright illustration. For example, if there are magazines or books on a table or posters on the wall in a photograph of a room, you do not need permission from the owners of the images used to make the magazines, or book jackets or posters.

The missing source

You must make all reasonable efforts to locate the owner of copyright material. If you know the author's name and the title of the work, you can try to locate the publisher through records kept in national libraries. For example, in Britain publishers must deposit a copy of every book in the British Library; and in the United States copyright owners must send two copies of their published works to the Copyright Office for deposit in the Library of Congress. Most copyright owners in America also register their published works at the Copyright Office, but in Britain there has been no register of copyright owners since December 1923.

When a book is out of print but still in copyright, write to the publisher, who should be able to redirect your inquiries to the author or author's agent. If the original publisher has gone out of business, you may be able to find out through the records of books in print whether the same title by the same author has joined the list of another publisher.

Write to the appropriate person or organization at the most recent address available. If you receive no reply, send a registered letter, which verifies your effort. In the event that you are still unsuccessful, it is usual to include a notice in the acknowledgements that permissions fees will be paid and acknowledgements given in reprints if the copyright owner comes forward.

Paying invoices

Occasionally, invoices are pro forma: you must pay them *before* permission is granted or prints and transparencies are supplied. More commonly, permission is granted on the condition that payment is made on publication. This sensible position reflects the understanding that quotations or illustrations can be dropped, and even an entire work cancelled, at any stage prior to publication.

Do everything you can to ensure that all fees for which the company is responsible are paid promptly.

- Keep all the invoices for a single project together, and check, code and pass them to the accounts department a month before payment is due.
- Remember, and remind accountants and your line manager if necessary, that copyright and reproduction permission are conditional on payment being made, and that the company may have to pay damages or the sale of the book might be delayed or halted if these rights are infringed.
- Remember, and remind accountants and your line manager if necessary, that cooperation from these *and other* sources in the future depends on the company having a reputation for prompt payment.

Acknowledgements

Sources should be acknowledged whether or not permission is required (see 'What's fair?', above). Acknowledgement can be made in the text, footnotes or end notes, under an illustration, in captions or lists of illustrations, in grouped acknowledgements and picture credits at the front or back of a publication.

Whenever permission is obtained, it is conditional on acknowledgement being made and in the wording specified by the grantor. It is not possible to impose consistency on acknowledgements from different sources; accuracy is the goal. If the permission has arrived too late for the required wording to be employed, write immediately to the source explaining what has happened and the wording that has been used.

Some grantors also make permission conditional on giving credit in a specific place. It is usual to give source notes for tables, charts, graphs and diagrams under the illustrations, but permission might also depend on them appearing in the list of acknowledgements. Photo agencies might request a credit on the same page as the picture, but for highly illustrated books most will agree to acknowledgement being made at the front or back of the volume. If you have to deviate from the position the source wants, as with wording, notify them immediately of what you plan to do.

11

Working with marketing,
sales and promotion

From the first stirrings of the idea to the passing of the final proofs, you are thinking about the readers, who they are and how to make the message attractive and accessible to them. Your co-workers in marketing, sales and promotion will be considering the same matters from a different perspective: how to make the targeted readers aware of the publication and how to get them to buy it.

As commissioning editor, you should be working with marketing and sales when you are evaluating the list and preparing proposals (see Chapter 2). The exchange of information at these times lays a foundation for what is to follow. By the time the proposal is accepted, you are in agreement about who the readers are, by what routes they will be reached, and what the sales targets are. But the house may publish hundreds of titles a year and the publication date for your proposals might be one or two years after the proposals are agreed. You — the commissioning, project and copy editors — have to continue to supply your colleagues with the materials they need, when they need them, so that they can do their jobs; and you have to maintain good communications so that you can do yours effectively.

The promotion department, too, will need information from you, particularly for the catalogue and for distribution of copies for review. For many books this is the only publicity planned. For others, there may be point-of-sale materials, author tours and launch parties. The decisions are not yours, but the information you provide might influence them. Be sure to remind the department of commitments in the author's contract, which should have been made only with their agreement.

Each of these departments will draw up schedules based on the estimated publication date of the books, so, as always, make sure you keep them informed of any delays or other occurrences that will affect the availability of proofs, jackets, bound copies or authors. Keep yourself and your authors informed, too, about plans for marketing and promoting the books.

Advance information sheet (AIS)

Most companies have standard formats for these initial notices of forthcoming books, which usually include:

- title and author,
- ISBN,
- specification,
- proposed publication date and price,
- a short blurb about the book,
- a short blurb about the author,
- a number of selling points.

Although they might be read by other people in the firm, AISs are prepared initially for the marketing, sales and promotion departments. Their purpose is to begin selling the titles: selling the ideas to your colleagues so that they can see how to sell the copies to the consumers. Later, AISs will be sent to retail outlets, and may be the only promotion some titles receive. All the information you are asked for is needed for good commercial reasons. The identification of the title and the specification need to be as complete and as accurate as possible, the blurbs and selling points focused not only on what is in the book but also on why readers will want it or need it. The closer you are to publication, the more accurate the basic information will be, but because an AIS is needed well in advance of publication to allow the other departments time to prepare the selling strategy and promotion, it may have to be prepared before the manuscript is available. When a book is not to be published until two or more years after contracted, so many other projects will have passed through your hands that you may find it difficult to remember the main selling points or to revive your earlier enthusiasm.

In either event, the AISs can be based on the information in the proposals. This is a simple matter when proposals have been written, but in many firms they are mainly oral, with estimates, synopses and sample chapters the only information on paper. The notes you made to guide you through presentations (see Chapter 2, page 29) will come in useful now too. However, it is even more effective to write AISs as soon as proposals have been accepted even if publication is a long time in the future. The arguments for publication, and your zeal, are at their freshest, and transforming the proposal into an information sheet will be relatively quick. Keep the form in the file until you need it. You can make minor revisions later, if they are needed — perhaps the title, price or publication date has changed — but if all the people involved are doing their jobs effectively, you will not have to make any major alterations.

Catalogues

The promotions department prepares catalogues to promote the next season's books, not merely to advertise current publications. It is important to the health of the entire list that the schedules for these books that sell books are maintained. Your role is to provide an entry for each of your titles on the date it is needed. Since the entries can be based on the information in the AISs, why is submitting catalogue copy on time often problematic? The usual answer is that it is not on your schedule. You have scheduled the books on which you are working, and catalogues are publications on which other people are working.

Put the dates by which the promotion department needs your copy on your global schedule. If you do not know the dates, ask. Then look at how many titles need blurbs by each of the cutoff dates. When you have a small number of entries to prepare, it might be easiest to do them all at once. It can help you to concentrate and develop a rhythm, and to avoid repetition. For the same reasons, when you have a large number of entries to prepare, it might be useful to divide them into small batches and work on them perhaps at weekly intervals; you can lose your concentration trying to do too many at once. Some people need a lot of time to write these little blurbs, others work best on a tight schedule. Whichever type you are, plan to have all your entries completed at least a week before the deadline. About two days before the deadline, reread them with a fresh eye and make any minor revisions necessary.

In writing catalogue copy, which often is shorter than jacket or cover blurb, avoid using superlatives. Unless you are publishing only one book in each category, none of them can be 'the best', 'the most' or 'the only one you'll ever need'. This kind of hype devalues other books on the list, and makes a poor impression on retailers and readers.

Especially in large firms, where entries are supplied by many editors, copywriters will revise your blurbs to achieve a consistent style, to avoid excessive repetition of the same adjectives and selling points, and to fit the copy into the space. Check the proofs to make sure that no inaccuracies have been inadvertently introduced.

Covers and jackets

Covers and jackets are important sales and marketing tools, not only because they appeal directly to the reader, as Chapter 6 makes clear, but also because they are used to sell the books to booksellers, which is why they must be prepared long in advance of publication day. The comments that the managers of all the departments involved in selling the books make at cover approval meetings reflect their knowledge and understanding of the impact that the submitted designs will have on the consumers. They will look at a design for what it says about the book, and they will see it in competition with other books in its market. Consulting sales and marketing colleagues before you brief designers can save everyone time and effort.

Although you brief covers individually, you can discuss them with sales and marketing in batches, perhaps monthly or quarterly, depending on how many there are. This might help you to see the general principles involved more clearly, and to streamline the consultation and briefing process a little more each time. Look at your global schedule to see which covers need to be briefed next. Arrange your meeting to allow everyone enough time to prepare and yourself enough time afterwards, perhaps several days, to absorb what has been said and incorporate it in your design briefs.

Use the AISs to focus your mind on the main selling points and jot down your briefing notes (see page 93), and questions you might have, in general or specific to each title. At the meeting, go through the projects one at a time. Mention the title and author, give a one-sentence summary of the content and list the main selling points. Then outline your brief for the cover and ask for your colleagues' perspective. They are not designers and you are not asking them for design ideas, but marketing and sales managers will be able to tell you:

- which selling points the design should reflect on the front and the back,
- the relative importance of the author's name, series title, book title, illustrations,
- whether they agree with the overall look you have suggested,
- whether special features, such as foil, shrinkwrapping, slipcases, bands or flashes are appropriate and advantageous,
- whether certain colours or colour combinations should be avoided.

As important to you as their views are their explanations. For each of these issues you want to know why. It might be perfectly clear, for example, that a white background will look shabby on display after a few days but a mystery why your colleagues do not want a green one; why on one book the series title should be more important than the volume title, and just the reverse on another; why shrinkwrapping is necessary or to be avoided; or why a film or TV tie-in is flashed on one front cover and a caption to an illustration on the back of another. You will also want to know whether their opinions are based on:

- observations of current fashions or trends in the market generally,
- the types of jacket produced by the competition for this title specifically,
- feedback on the covers of similar books in last season's list,
- personal taste.

The result of this meeting might be that you will want to review all the covers and jackets that your company produced last season, look at those of your main competitors or visit a large bookshop and see the impact jackets have on you as a consumer. Having widened your own perspective, you are in a better position to weigh and interpret the comments of your colleagues while finalizing your briefs for the designers.

Blurbs

The front of the jacket or cover should attract attention, and the copy on flaps, if available, and the back should hook the readers' interest and make them want to look inside. Traditionally, the copy on front flap and back jacket are about the book, and the back flap has a biographical sketch of the author. On books that have covers only, all this selling copy is on the back. Neither the flaps nor the back should ever be left blank. Conversely, do not run text from the front to the back flap. Flaps are read mainly by people standing in bookshops, for whom flipping the entire contents of a book mid-sentence is awkward: they will not do it, and the selling copy does not get a fair chance to do its job.

Fiction has the advantage that the characters and plot of each novel are unique, at least to some extent, and you can play upon those unique aspects to create a blurb that excites interest. It should not tell the story or give too much detail about the characters; its purpose is to create a mood that captures the reader's attention and makes them want to know more. Even when the author's name is a greater draw than the theme of the book, blurbs whet the appetite and may encourage the reader to buy *now*.

Nonfiction can be more difficult. Describing the content is necessary but not enough. Most subject areas are packed with competition, and for each of your titles you have to assemble the selling points to convince readers to buy this book rather than one of the others. You might, of course, have a more or less captive audience. You may think that students or practitioners who need the latest book in their field or the only one on a particular specialism do not need to be sold a book, they need to buy it. None the less, the blurb has to tell readers why they should buy *this* book, because where there is one, there will be others, and the latest will not be the last.

The selling points should be well established by the time blurbs have to be written: they convinced the company to accept the proposal and they have been reiterated in the AIS. Most author's questionnaires ask authors to describe their book and provide an autobiographical sketch. Good ones explain that this information will be used for promotion and marketing, and ask authors to summarize the content of their book, highlighting its main features and benefits, and to list their qualifications and credentials for writing it. Your knowledge of the market, the competition and the book itself will help you decide which aspects to emphasize.

'This book' is an opening phrase to avoid; it is dull and uninviting. It might be the way you start assembling your thoughts in a draft, but do not allow it to reach print. Not everyone who picks up a book intends to buy it; the blurb's job is to convince them. To have a chance of doing that the first line must grab the readers' attention so that they continue reading. Look for an angle. Ask yourself what is so wonderful, exciting, necessary, new, revolutionary or entertaining, about this book and why the readers will benefit from buying it. Go into a large bookshop and read some blurbs at random; what makes some interesting and others boring?

Still having a difficult time? Ask your colleagues in promotion for some hints, and see if you can find a book or a course on copywriting. After you have written a blurb, ask someone else to read it and give you some feedback. Reread it yourself a few days later. Try to be objective. Never mind if it was the best you thought you could do at the time, does it work? If not, try again.

It should be clear that you must plan enough time for blurb-writing, and rewriting if necessary, and put it on your schedule. There is no standard: some people produce the right quality material quickly, others more slowly. Know yourself.

For the sake of sales and so that you can sleep at night, check at every stage of proof that the ISBN on the jacket or cover is the same as the one inside the book.

Blads

Blads are eight- or sixteen-page samplers of an illustrated book produced for promotional purposes. Within this short extent they must show the typical appearance and range of material, as well as the list of contents, the specifications and estimated price and publication date. Some blads are produced before the project is commissioned, to help secure co-edition deals; all are produced before the book is in proof. Despite this, the text and illustrations must be those that will appear in the finished book. Producing blads without disrupting or delaying the progress of the books requires good organization and careful scheduling: find out when blads will be required, and work out the timing backwards from then. Producing blads that do their job well requires effective communication with the people who are going to use them.

Consult the appropriate colleagues in the rights department if the blad is to be used for co-edition sales. Show them the rough layouts and draw their attention to those features that are important to potential publishing partners, such as the typographical design that makes your own edition attractive and allows languages of different lengths to fit into the same space as well; and the size, nature and number of colour illustrations. Do not simply wait for feedback, ask for it. The purpose of the consultation is to find out if there is anything in the blad that will preclude or hinder co-edition sales, so that the pages, and even the grid, can be altered.

Similarly, show the blad layouts to the marketing, sales and promotions managers. Draw their attention to how the blad exemplifies the book's selling points, and ask for feedback.

Discuss the outcome of your consultations with the designer. Pass on the positive comments and together consider what changes can be made to overcome any criticism.

Sales conferences

These dates are among the first vertical lines you put on your global schedule. The publication dates that fall after the conference are those of the titles that will be presented. Some commissioning editors ask project managers and desk editors to make a number of the presentations, providing them with an opportunity to be involved with sales directly and to give the books on which they have been working a good send-off. By this time there should be a battery of sales tools available: the AIS, the jacket and information about the author at least, and perhaps a blad or some proofs.

As always, prepare yourself. First, find out how much time you will be given to make your presentations, and then decide how much time you will give to each title. It is unlikely that you will divide the time evenly; some titles are more important or need more of a push than others.

Next, check that you have all the basic tools, and take steps to get missing items. Look through what you have and decide if you need or can make use of other available material; for example, sales figures for other books in the series or by the same author, the number of students enrolled annually on a particular course, statistics that show a growing interest in the subject. Review the author's questionnaires to see if there are any points about their activities or where they live that will help the sales team to get the books into the shops. Consider if the authors of any of your more important titles would be effective and entertaining presenters. If so, suggest them to the sales manager. However, be sure to discourage attempts to invite authors, even those of your most important books, who are poor communicators: they may inadvertently dampen enthusiasm.

Now, use your tools to prepare the presentations. You might be delivering only a few, but the salesforce will be listening to many, so they need to be attention-grabbing and memorable; which means concise, focused, well organized and varied. They should include:

- a brief description of the content,
- the main selling points in order of importance — a good opportunity for visual aids,
- relevant details about the author,
- relevant information about the series,
- the nature of the competition.

You might enliven some presentations with an amusing anecdote about the book or the author, but keep it short. And whether relating an amusing tale or describing the book, be accurate. If a story or a sales point needs to be exaggerated to have effect, drop it.

When your material is ready, prepare your performance. Looking down and reading from a script or whispering is not an effective way to sell your books. Rehearse aloud. Start by introducing yourself if no one is going to do it for you, or by saying hello, and then read your presentations. Concentrate on what you are saying, not how you are feeling. Do this several times. It helps you to learn your material and to get used to the sound of your own voice in an otherwise quiet room. When you feel familiar with the presentations, note the main points for each title on an index card; they are easier to refer to than pieces of paper. Repeat them again, trying not to rely on your notes. It does not matter if you do not say everything exactly the way you first wrote it, as long as you cover the main points. Even if you have to look at your notes occasionally, you will feel confident that you are prepared, which can help you to relax.

Talk to the individual members of the salesforce. You might get some feedback on titles being presented by you and other editors, learn about progress or problems with recently published titles, or hear some news about your competitors. You will also begin to develop a relationship with colleagues whose job it is to sell the books on which you have worked.

It wasn't my idea

You might have to prepare blurbs or presentations for books that you did not commission, because you have taken over from another person or because you are a project editor or copy-editor. At whatever stage in the process you begin, however limited your knowledge or involvement, write only what you know to be true. If you do not know enough, you can find out more, but never bluff, never make claims that you cannot support. Other people expect to act on what you say, and your false trails can damage the authors' books and your relationship with your colleagues.

Now you will appreciate how useful it is for commissioning editors to prepare the AISs when the projects are initiated, for they can be used as briefs not only for preparing other sales material but also for working on the book itself. Alas, it is not always so. Many editors have to pick up projects with no background information other than specifications and estimates. Yes, there really are people who manage not to leave comprehensive written evidence of a project's inception — no letters, memos or synopses. Perhaps they were not very well organized or efficient, and that is why they are gone; or perhaps they took these documents as souvenirs.

Still, you have the specifications and maybe even the manuscripts now. You might be able to tell what the books are about and who the intended readers are. If not, and to fill in other gaps in your knowledge, contact the authors as soon as you take over their projects. They will understand that you cannot know about their title in the same detail as their original commissioning editor, and they will probably be aware if that person was disorganized. Even in a short conversation they should be able to give you a clear idea of their book. Follow this up by getting them to complete an author's questionnaire immediately, no matter how far in the future publication is; it provides you with information about them and their views on the selling points of their book. This will help you to develop the author–editor relationship as well as to prepare blurbs.

Parties and tours

Launch parties and author tours of bookshops for signing sessions are to promote and sell books, and marketing and promotion departments will decide when they are relevant. You play your part in selling the books and the authors to these colleagues initially and keeping them informed of developments. When there is to be a party or a tour, your job will be to liaise with the promotions department, providing background on the authors, and with the authors, explaining what the plans are and what is expected of them. The promotions department and authors might then work together quite closely, and you will retain your supporting role.

For authors whose books do not merit this treatment, acknowledgement of their achievement in some way on publication day — a congratulatory note or phone call — would, no doubt, be welcome, particularly if you can say that you have seen copies on display. If your books are not sold in bookshops but by direct mail or into schools, you can send your message earlier, when sending the authors their complimentary copies. It brings a long process to a nice conclusion, and may lay the foundation for future collaboration.

Glossary

acknowledgements There are two kinds: optional and obligatory. The first is the authors' public expression of gratitude for all those who helped them in bringing the book into being; if it is omitted, some people might be offended. The second is given whenever copyright material is used, even when permission is not needed; if it is omitted, copyright is infringed — a very serious mistake.

authors The people who create the work: writers, illustrators, photographers, translators, indexers. Treat them all professionally, with respect, and help them get their message to the readers.

authors' disks The electronic form of the manuscript, which can streamline the production process if authors are briefed and follow the brief, and if the level of editing is minimal. Otherwise, useful only for printing out the hard copy.

blad A booklet of representative pages of an illustrated book, this domestic and rights sales tool must be scheduled carefully in order not to disrupt progress of the book.

blues *See* Ozalid

blurb If you don't have a natural talent for writing this promotional copy about the book and the author, work hard; it's the second thing that consumers look at when deciding whether to buy the book; *see also* jacket.

budget The amount of money that can be spent affects and is affected by every aspect of your job. Think of it as a high cliff: you don't want to go over it.

bulk The thickness of a book, which some consumers equate with value and which production controllers can manipulate for you.

colour proofs Proofs of colour illustrations, tints for boxes and decorative devices. They should be corrected with an understanding of what is practicable, not with a demand for perfection.

communication The purpose of our industry, and the lack of which is responsible for most of its problems. Take control: initiate and maintain communication.

copyright Must be protected; must not be infringed; make sure you understand and fulfil your responsibilities in both areas.

cover Holds the book together and, when there is no jacket, makes the first impression on potential consumers; *see also* jacket.

CRC Camera-ready copy: text and black line artwork that is printed on bromide because it is ready to be turned into film for printing. If it is not ready, it is not CRC. If you find something that needs to be changed because it would affect sales, endanger readers or break the law, examine your procedures to see how such a serious error got to this stage.

direct costs Those editorial, design and production costs that are allocated to producing the book. This is the budget you see; *see also* overheads.

DTP Desktop publishing; the use of computers to generate text, typesetting, page make-up and origination of illustrations. A useful tool, not a substitute for knowledge and skill, nor an excuse to make endless changes because you don't get a bill from an external supplier; *see also* overheads.

dummy Made to dimensions of proposed book and used to show paper, bulk and style of binding; the only time there should be consecutive blank pages in a book.

fixed costs Those editorial, design and production costs that do not change whether you produce one or 1 million copies.

galleys The first proofs of typesetting. Although there will always be some mistakes to correct, this is not an opportunity for authors to rewrite or for editors to re-edit.

global schedule One that enables you to see your entire workload and the external factors affecting it at a glance; a tool for control and stress-free work.

grid The template for page design, a framework for visual consistency, it can be flexible in the hands of good designers, and should be understood by editors.

gross margin An indication of the profits a book would make if only they weren't subject to overheads.

jacket The first part of the book that consumers see, which might influence them to look more closely; it's a sales tool — use it; *see also* blurb.

leading The space between the lines of type, it affects the number of lines on a page and the ease with which they can be read.

market *n.* The intended consumers, as groups of people and countries; *see also* readers. *v.* How sales will be directed at these intended consumers.

mark-up For commissioning editors, the factor by which the unit cost is multiplied to produce the price, or by which a price can be divided to indicate the acceptable unit cost. For other editors, designers and production controllers, the codes used to indicate the nature of typesetting.

net margin The 'bottom line' on a proposal form.

origination The process of turning artwork and photographs into film for printing.

overheads The costs of running the company that are borne equally by all titles. This is the budget you don't see; it includes staff salaries, which are calculated on estimated productivity, so if you don't do your job in the time allowed, you increase the overheads — in effect, go over budget. If DTP costs are hidden in the overheads, it is not easy to see how misuse — repeated and extensive changes — is gradually pushing up the costs of all books until it is too late.

Ozalid The proof of the final film; do not read it, do not even think of making any changes to it, just check it for completeness and position.

pages Allow authors to proofread only if this is the first stage of proofs, and warn them about making any alterations that would affect pagination.

quality Ranges from high to low and should always be deliberate; part of the equation with budget and schedule.

readers The people at whom books are aimed, whose mindset you must understand and adopt to help make the authors' message clear.

repro house Where colour images are originated; *see also* origination.

schedule The timetable for producing work, a driving force for everything you do; put yourself in the driver's seat or be driven.

unit cost The cost of producing a single copy; can be deceptive if editorial, design and, especially, DTP costs are concealed in the overheads.

variable costs Those costs that depend on the number of copies produced, also called manufacturing costs.

Index

Numerals in italics refer to figures.

acknowledgements 154, 157
  and fair dealing 153
  prepared by picture researcher 101, 113
acquisitions editors 2
advance information sheets (AIS) 160, 162
  based on proposal information 160
  usefulness of 162, 167
advertising by and for freelancers 132
agents, developing relationships with 33
artistic works, copyright in 146–7, 149–51
  see also copyright; moral rights
artists *see* illustrators
artwork
  briefing 89–91, *90*
  checking 91
  schedule for 67–8
  see also illustrations
assessing
  the list 7, *8*, 9–11
  manuscripts 35, 36–7, 60–3
  projects 44–67
author tours 167
authors 19–23
  accuracy of information from 75
  acknowledgement on publication
    day 167
  briefing for 31–2
  budget problems created by
    and changes to proof 76, 125
  checking roughs 91
  and copy-editing 73–6; *see also*
    copy-editing
  and copyright *see* copyirght
  dates for receiving and returning
    proofs 67
  established 21–2
  explaining contract to 32–3
  ideas in search of 22–3

  and indexes 78
  new to the publishing house 21–2
  nurturing 33–5
  and picture research 105
  query response time 65–6
  requesting permissions 153, 154
  and revisions to draft manuscript 23, 37
  and schedules 31, 32
  submissions from unpublished 20–1
author's questionnaires 163, 167
author's style, paying attention to 71–3

balanced list
  creation of 14–15
  keeping track of performance 16
Berne Convention for the Protection
  of Literary and Artistic Works 149
  see also copyright
binding style, influence of 87
blads
  co-edition sales tool 164–5
  and copy-editing schedule 68, 77
  and picture research schedule 107, 109
  and project schedule 49
blurbs 161, 163–4
book-club editions 12
briefing
  artwork 89–91, *90*
  authors 31–2
  basic 37
  colleagues, by commissioning
    editor 37–9
  copy-editors 52–3, 60–3
  on covers 162
  designers 85–95; *see also* designers
  freelancers 137–8
  indexers 78–80
  photography 91–2

picture researchers 102–6
potential authors 22
principles of 37–9
proofreaders 53
scheduling time for 67–8
shortcomings of, give personal
    feedback 57
briefs, assimilation of 60–3
budgets 58
    assessing annual 15
    creating, for individual titles 25–6, *26*
    for design, maintenance of 96
    for freelance work 139–42
    for picture researchers 110–11
    principles of 11–14, *12, 13*
    production, maintenance of 123–5
    revising 27–9
    and schedules 13
    see also costs

cast-off
    by designer 83–4
    rough, by editor 62–3
catalogue copy 49, 161
catalogues 161
changes
    affecting production 121, 126
    author's, on proofs 55–6
    authors' agreement for 74–5
    consult with production before
        making 123–4
    in picture research brief 111
    unplanned 76
checking
    for accuracy of information 75
    copy-editing 54–5
    pages 96–8
    proofreading 55
co-editions 12, 76–7
    coordinating schedules for 49, 77
    editing text for 77
    experienced designers for 85
    planning of and pitfalls in 24
co-publishers, needs of 77
colour
    advice from designers 87
    proofs 98–9
commissioning 7–29
commissioning editors 1–2, 4–5
    assessing manuscripts 35, 36–7, 38

and author selection 19–23
briefing colleagues 37–9, *38*
checking competition 10–11
and co-editions 24
and the completed manuscripts 36–7, 46
and feedback from colleagues 37,
    45–6, 76
and influence on author
    development 33–5
and list analysis 7, *8*, 9–11, 14–15
prepare advance information sheets
    (AIS) 167
providing feedback 38
and schedules 16–18, *17*, 35, 36
working with designers 87–8
working with marketing and sales 159
working with production 117, *118–9*,
    119–21, *122*, 123–4
see also ideas
communication
    and authors 20, 33–5
    essential and effective 5–6, 22, 26
    importance of 2
compensation, to freelancers if project
    cancelled 110–11, 139
competition from other publishers 10–11
completeness
    of page layouts 97
    of project materials 61
complexity of project materials 61
consistency of page layouts 97
constructive criticism 56
    see also feedback
contingency allowance
    in freelance budget 141
    never remove 29
    in production estimate 121, 123
contingency time 18
    for colleagues with time problems 68
    copy-editing 65, 66
contracts 32–3, 36
conventions in page layout 97
copy-editing 3, 59–80
    author's style 71–3
    checking of 54–5
    co-editions 76–7
    first edit and mark-up 65
    principles of 70–6
    and proofreading 3
    rules and alternatives 70–1

copy-editors 3–4, 5
  advice to commissioning editors
    concerning changes 76
  assessing manuscripts 60–3
  briefing of 52–3
  choice of 51
  establish a relationship with the
    author 73–4
  freelance, stages of engagement 136
  how not to antagonize the author 74–6
  inexperienced, supervised 53
  other responsibilities 52–3
  planning ahead on global schedule
    chart 63–5
  principles for 59–60
  role of, on queries/comments 75–6
  treating authors with care and
    consideration 73–4
  viewing the smaller picture 4–5
  working with others 5
copyright 145–52
  Berne Convention 149
  duration of, in different
    countries 149, 153
  duration of, literacy, dramatic and
    artistic work in the UK and US *146–7*
  exists as soon qualifying original work is
    created 145, 148
  fair use/fair dealing 150, 151–3
  giving notice of 148
  infringement of 150, 153
  ownership and rights 149–51
  Universal Copyright Convention 149
Copyright Act 1976 (USA) 145, *147*
Copyright, Designs and Patents Act
  1988 (UK) 145, *146*
  moral rights in 151
copyright material
  in anthologies 152
  in databases, multimedia and other
    electronic publications 154
  use of 61
copyright registration 156
costs
  correction 13
  fixed and variable 120–1
  see also direct costs; fixed costs;
    manufacturing costs; production costs
covers and jackets 92–5, 161–65
  briefing the designers 84, 93–5, *94*

  information on 163
  and marketing and sales 161–3
  preliminary designs 93, 95
  schedule for 49
cover approval meetings 161–62
covering letters
  from agents 20
  from prospective authors 20
  to freelancers 137
credits *see* acknowledgements
critical path analysis
  of complete publishing process 47, *116*
  revealing a too tight schedule 68–9
cross-referencing 61, 79

delegated work, checking of 54–6
delegation 51–3
design brief 85–9
designers
  briefing stylists 92
  briefing for covers 84, 93–5
  briefing for project 38, 85, *86*, 87–8
  categorized list of illustrations 89
  and commissioned photography
    84, 88, 91
  consultations regarding schedules 95–6
  cooperating with production
    controllers 88–9
  discussions of colour proofs with 99
  handing over manuscripts, disks and
    illustrations to 95
  the index 79
  instructions for 38
  job titles of 84
  jobs not done by 82–3
  responsibilities of 83–4
  working with 91–9
  see also artwork; covers and jackets;
    photography
desktop publishing (DTP) 25, 115, 117
  in-house, still a cost 127
direct costs 12
  include costs for freelance work 139
disks from authors 37, 88–9, 127
  checking, for compatibility 62
  date for receipt of 31–2
  handing over 95, 127–8
  unusable, effect of 123
drafts materials
  appraisal of 37, 44–6

date for 31–2
feedback to commissioning editor 45

editorial changes, cost of 127
editorial and design
fixed costs 120
time and money 25–6
editors
freelance, untried 133
general, for multi-author works 32
see also commissioning editors;
copy-editors; project management;
project managers
endpapers, production evaluation
of costs 121
entries for indexes 79
estimate requests 23, 24
see also costs; production costs;
production estimate request form
expenditure budget 15
see also budgets
expenses, reimbursed to freelancers 141

fair use/fair dealing 150, 151–3
feedback 6, 14, 24, 56–7, 58
to commisioning editors 76
on editorial and design work 38–9
to freelancers 142
from presentations 166
to authors 22–3, 37
fees for freelancers 140–1
fiction 1, 163
financial savings from using
freelancers 130
first edit and mark up 65–6
first proofs, reading and collating 67
fixed costs, editorial and
design 25, *26*
flair and imagination in
commissioning 7
flat-plans 84
formal meetings 6
format and filling, work of the
designer 87–8
format publishing, designer
involvement 81–2
'freebies' 12
freelance organizations 131–2
freelance records 134, *135*
freelance work, growth in 129

freelancers
briefing of 52–3, 137–8, *138*
budgets for work of 139–42
building a team of 134–5
checking work of 139
copy-editors 136
copy-editors and proofreaders,
choosing 51–2, 130–3, 136–7
feedback to 142
in-house view of 132–3
indexers, briefing 78–80
judged by original letters 132–3
keeping records of 134–5, *135*
maintaining good relations with 143
picture researchers 110–11
reasons for use 129–30
scheduling of 135–7
sources of 130–2
stages in engagement of 136
training 70
views on editors and companies
134, 143
working with 129–43
writing to publishing houses 130–1
Friday schedules 68

gap-filling 14, 15
global schedules
and artwork and photography 89, 95–6
and authors 35, 36
and blurbs 49, 164
creating basic 16, *17*, 18
and draft materials 35
and copy-editors 63, *64*, 65–9
and freelancers 135–7
and managing editors 57–8
and picture research, jackets
and blads 49, 106–9
and promotion copy 161
and project editors 47, 49, *50*, 51
and sales conferences 16, 165
graphs and charts, copyright for 152
grid creation 83

handover dates 68
handover forms
editors and designers 39, *40–1*
for freelancers 137
proofreaders 53
handover meetings 39, 53

hard copy and disk 62
holding fees 110
house style 71, 75
  for indexes 80

ideas
  development of 18–19
  finding 1, 2, 7
  sales potential of 23–4
  in search of authors 22–3
  selling 2, 24, 29
  strengthening 27
illustrated books
  co-editions 24, 76–7
  creating and developing ideas for 18–19
  designer involvement in 82
  format, extent and type 19
  picture research fees 155
  see also designers, illustrations,
    picture research
illustration-text manipulation,
  by designer 87
illustrations
  breakdown for designer 88
  colour proofs 98–9
  exclusive rights to reproduction 149
  fair use/fair dealing 153
  for co-editions 77
  handing over 95, 127–8
  incidental inclusion 155
  manipulation of 28
  owned first by creating illustrators and
    photographers 150–1
  placement of 97
  and price 28
  and production 120
  see also artwork; photographs; picture list
illustrators
  briefs for 89–91
  buying copyright from 150
  commissioning of 84
in-house experience of freelancers 132–3
indexers, briefing of 78–80
indexes
  entries for 79
  number and kind 78–9
  presentation of 80
  value of 78
information sources 75
ISBNs, keep checking 164

jackets *see* covers and jackets
job titles 1, 3, 4

late publication 11,13
launch parties 167
list-builders 1–2
  see also commissioning editors
literary and dramatic works,
  rights of copyright owner in 149

management styles 43–4, 57–8, 130
managing editors 4
  delegation of project management 57–8
  see also commissioning editors;
    project managers
manufacturing costs 120
manuscripts
  assessment of 35–7, 38, 60–3
  attached handover form 39
  conversion to books 3–4
  copy-editing in-house 49
  delivery on time by author 31
  determining length of 62–3
  handing over 95, 127–8
  overlength, cost/price implications of
    46–7
  presentation of 61–2
  underlength 36
mark-up 12–13, *13*
market forces and pay for freelancers 140
marketing issues 9
markets, influencing types of
  illustration 103
materials, sending and receiving 127–8
meeting rooms 6
meetings, effective 6
moral rights 151
multi-author works
  consistent tone, anonymous voice 71–3
  general editor for 32

negative feedback 56
negotiation over contracts 32–3
net profit margin 12
networking 21–2
nonfiction, blurbs for 163

origination, of non-fiction 1–2
overheads 58
  a percentage of turnover 12
overtime 69–70

page layouts 84
  checking of 96–8
  problems and solutions 98
paper, production controller's
  knowledge of 120
paperback editions, rights for 2
payment, to freelancers 137, 140–2
permissions 61, 153–6
  and acknowledgements,
    recording of 153, *153*
  given in writing 154
  paying invoices for 156
  picture 101, 155
  requests for 154, *155*
  terms and conditions of 156, 157
photographers, freelance,
  and copyrights 150–1
photographs
  care and control of 111–12
  copyright and reproduction fees 155
  picture researcher's responsibilities 101
  preliminary and final selection of 106–7
  see also acknowledgements, illustrations
photography, commissioned 88
  briefing 91–2
  checking 92
  and designer's role 84
picture credits *see* acknowledgements
picture list
  author's contributions to 105
  changes to 111
  essential content and omissions 104
  images for jacket and blad 106
  requirements for colour and format 105
picture research, schedules and procedures
  67, 106–10
picture researchers
  brief for 102–6, *102*, 111
  contract for *108–9*
  fees for 110–11
  in-house 103
  responsibilities of 101, *108*
  returning materials 107
  and schedule 110
  working with 101–13
pitfalls in co-editions 24
planning 14, 63
positive feedback 56
post-mortems, constructive
  uses of 13–14

presentation
  of project materials 61–2
  of indexes 80
presentations to sales conferences 165–6
prices 9, 10, 15
  related to cost and profit margin
    11, 12–13
  too high 27–8
production 11, 12, 13, 115
  involvement in project 117
  receipt of materials from 128, *128*
  schedules, maintaining stages of 126
  sending and receiving materials
    127–8, *128*
  to be informed of changes 123–4
production costs 11, 12, 13, 117
  final estimate of 123
  first estimate of 121
  fixed and variable 120
  influenced by use of DTP or
    conventional typesetting 25
production editor 3
production estimate form 121, *122*
production estimate request form 117,
  118–19, 119
production route
  decided before proposal acceptance 127
  and influence on costs 25
production schedules 47, *48, 126*
profit margin 11, *11*, 13, 23
  affected by changes 124
profits, need for 12
project assessment
  early appraisal 44–6
  full-term delivery 46
project management
  assessing the project 44–7
  maintaining budgets 58
  checking 54–6
  delegating 51–3
  providing feedback 56–7
  scheduling 47–51, 58
  styles of 43–4, 57–8
project managers
  briefing for 38
  building a freelance team 134
  checking freelance work in progress 139
  checking page layouts 96–8
  checking photography 92
  communicating with colleagues 121

and the completed manuscript 46–7, 66
and the copy-editor 59–70
freelance, reporting and
    submitting materials 139
main responsibilities of 43–4
working with designers 81–99
working with freelancers 129–43
working with marketing,
    sales and promotion 159–67
working with picture researchers 101–13
working with production 115–28
project materials, examination by
    copy-editor 61–3
project proposals
    cutting the spec 28–9
    justifying the price 27–8
    outline to managing editor and
        design manager 25
    presentation and acceptance 29
    revision of 27–9
    strengthening ideas 27
    working with marketing and sales 159
promotions department 167
    information needed 159
    using advance information sheets
        (AIS) 160
proof corrections 124–5
proof-return form *128*
proofreaders
    briefing of 53
    choice of 51–2
    freelance, untried 133
proofreading 3
    checking of 55
publication dates 26, 29
publicity, use of pictures for 107
publisher's lists
    avoid competition within 10
    analysis of own 7–9, 14
    check competing 10–11
    foundations of 9–14
    strengths and weaknesses of 9

reference materials/handbooks,
    for copy-editing 70–1
reliability of authors 22
retail sales price (RSP), positions a book
    in the market 12
rights managers 13
    check on sales potential 23

roughs 89
    checking of 91
    see also artwork

sales conferences 165–6
sales manager, on sales potential 23
sales and marketing 10, 167
    discussion of covers with 162
    feedback on authors 21
    working with 159–67
sales performance of published list 9
sales potential of new proposals 23–4
sample chapters 20–1
schedules 26
    affecting author contact 74
    and blad 49
    for blurb writing 164
    complicated by co-editions 77
    disruption by outside events 49, 51
    DTP *48*
    and freelancers 135–7
    and illustrated books *48*
    and indexes 80
    from marketing, sales
        and promotions 159
    maintenance of 95, 126
    management of 57–8
    and missing material 61
    and procedures for picture
        research 106–10
    and project assessment 45
    too tight, actions to consider 68–9
    traditional production *48*
    also see global schedules, scheduling
scheduling
    for commissioning 16–18
    copy-editing 63–70
    of freelancers 135–7
    for project management 47–51
second edit, time for 66
sources, missing 157
specifications
    cutting to reduce costs 28–9
    improvement of 27–8
    for picture researcher *102*, 103
spot checking 55
subeditors 3
subentries in indexes 79
subsidiary rights, income from 11, 12, 23
'surely you mean', never to be used 75–6

synopses
  requested from potential authors 22
  reveal much about authors 20

targeting readers 159
text
  evaluation of quality and editability 45
  examined by copy-editor 62
text length 27–8
time, saved by employing
  freelancers 129–30
timescales, agreement on 29
training 14, 70
typography, planned by designer 83

unit cost 12–13, *13*

United Kingdom Copyright, Designs and
  Patents Act 1988 145, 146, 149, 151
  United States Copyright Act 1976
    145, *147*, 149
Universal Copyright Convention
  (UCC) 149
  see also copyright

visual approach, communicate
  to designer 87–8
volume rights, permission for 154

weak areas in lists 14–15
working relationships, building of 39
world rights, permission for 154
writing, as a creative process 73